THE **DIVE SITES** OF
MAURITIUS

ALAN MOUNTAIN

 **PASSPORT BOOKS**
NTC/Contemporary Publishing Company

This edition published in 1997 by
Passport Books
An imprint of NTC/Contemporary Publishing Company
4255 West Touhy Avenue, Lincolnwood (Chicago), Illinois, 60646-1975
U.S.A.

International Standard Book Number: 0-8442-4859-2
Library of Congress Catalog Card Number: 97-67404

First published in the UK in 1995 by
New Holland (Publishers) Ltd
London • Cape Town • Sydney • Singapore

Managing editor: Mariëlle Renssen
Editor: Brenda Borchert
Concept design: Philip Mann
Design and DTP: Peter Bosman
Design concept: Peter Bosman
Map DTP: Renée Barnes
Trace guides: Lellyn Creamer

Reproduction by Unifoto (Pty) Ltd, Cape Town
Printed and bound by Tien Wah Press (Pte) Ltd, Singapore

Photographic Acknowledgements:
All photographs are by Alan Mountain except: page 58 Kurt Amsler (Photo Access); pages 94, 95 Christian Bossu-Picat (L'ile aux Images); back cover, title page, pages 4, 24, 37, 53, 62, 83, 89 (top and bottom), 102-103, 104, 107, 116 John Brazendale; pages 77, 78 Geremy Cliff; page 50 Wolfgang Grülke; page 71 Dennis King; front cover inset, pages 16, 18, 65 Herman Potgieter; pages 13, 15, 17, 22-23, 40, 52, 64, 66, 82 Alain Proust (Struik Image Library); front cover, pages 45, 67, 72, 74, 97 Jürgen Seier; pages 28, 101 David Steele (Photo Access); page 80 Patrick Wagner (Photo Access).

Publisher's Acknowledgements

The Publisher would like to thank marine life consultant, Professor Mike Bruton, formerly Director of the JLB Smith Institute of Ichthyology and now Director of Education and Scientific Services at the Two Oceans Aquarium, Victoria and Alfred Waterfront, Cape Town, as well as the JLB Smith Institute of Ichthyology in Grahamstown, in particular Doctor Phil Heemstra and Margaret Crampton, and Professor Charles Griffiths of the Zoology Department at the University of Cape Town, for their kind assistance in the production of this book.

Author's Acknowledgements

I would like to thank Yves Halbwachs for his help
while I was in Mauritius and afterwards.
Special thanks are due to Yann von Arnim, who gave generously
and unhesitatingly of his time and profound knowledge on Mauritian marine life.
To Hugues Vitry, who gave me a taste of the fascination underwater
Mauritius can offer the patient observer and for unquestioningly lending me
his camera when mine jammed.
Similar thanks are due to Thierry de Chazal who lent me his strobe when mine was
damaged after an accident, and for all the information and assistance he gave me.
Finally, I would like to thank the many professional divers who shared their knowledge
with me and who took me to see some of Nature's marine gems.
In particular I would like to mention Pierre Szalay, Kevin Cock, Pappy Bordie, Karl
Heinz and Marie-Christine Berger, Alain Randiame, Uwe Ertl, Emanuele Senatore,
Jean-Marc Thevenau, Mike Frederic, Raymond Lai-Cheong, Henri Autard, Nasser
Beeharry and Anthony Pierre. I apologize for not mentioning the many other people
who also helped to make this book possible.

CONTENTS

HOW TO USE THIS BOOK

THE SUBREGIONS

The dive sites included in this book are arranged within six main geographical areas, or subregions of Mauritius. An introduction to the individual subregions describes the key characteristics and features of these main areas, as well as the general diving conditions that prevail. Background information on climate, environment, points of interest and advantages or disadvantages to diving in the subregions are also provided.

THE MAPS

The introduction to the dive sites section of this book effectively illustrates the breakdown of the six subregions into which Mauritius has been divided.

Each of the dive site subregions is subsequently illustrated by an enlarged, detailed map of the specific area. The purpose of the map is to easily identify the location of the dive sites described: this is achieved by repeating the number in the dive sites section, and on the map. For example:

1 will cross-reference to both the map and the dive site.

As most diving in Mauritius is organized through centres which operate from hotels, the maps indicate the hotels from which the diver can access the site. The coral reef surrounding the island is indicated, as are lighthouses, wrecks, major towns and places of special interest. The map legend illustrated below pertains to all maps used in this book.

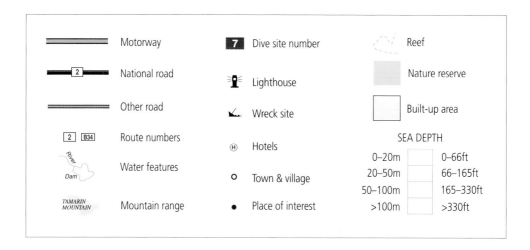

Motorway	**7** Dive site number	Reef
National road	Lighthouse	Nature reserve
Other road	Wreck site	Built-up area
2 B34 Route numbers	(H) Hotels	SEA DEPTH
Water features	o Town & village	0–20m 0–66ft / 20–50m 66–165ft / 50–100m 165–330ft
TAMARIN MOUNTAIN Mountain range	• Place of interest	>100m >330ft

THE DIVE SITE DESCRIPTIONS

Each region's premier dive sites are listed and begin with a number corresponding to the relevant map, a star rating, and symbols indicating key information (*see* below) pertaining to that site. Critical practical details (i.e. location, access, conditions and average and maximum depths) precede the description of the site, its marine life and special points of interest.

THE STAR-RATING SYSTEM

Each site has been awarded a rating, with a maximum of five and a minimum of one star.

★ pertains to scuba diving, and

☆ to snorkelling, as follows:

★★★★★	first class
★★★★	highly recommended
★★★	good
★★	average
★	poor

THE REGIONAL DIRECTORIES

At the end of each subregion in the dive sites section is a regional directory with helpful telephone numbers and addresses, largely relating to diving centres which operate in Mauritius, but also containing other interesting snippets of information.

OTHER FEATURES OF THIS BOOK

• Each section of the book is colour coded for ease of reference, as per the contents page.
• A general introduction to Mauritius will fill you in on historical details of the island, and tell you a bit about the people and the economy of the island. This is followed by travelling tips – how to get to Mauritius and how to get around the island once you are there. There is a wealth of information on diving and snorkelling in each region.
• Boxes containing interesting tips and concise information on certain species of marine life exist throughout the text.
• Feature spreads on special items of interest such as the island of Rodrigues, turtles and sharks are combined in the dive site text to make this a wholly informative and interesting book which no diver should be without.

INTRODUCING MAURITIUS

Physical Features

The island of Mauritius was once an active volcano that formed part of a chain of volcanoes stretching from Réunion in the south (where there is still an active volcano) to the Seychelles in the north. Over many millions of years the ancient volcano has been eroded, leaving jagged Matterhorn-like mountains, piles of volcanic rock and a few craters as reminders of its early origin. The pear-shaped island covers 1865km^2 (1159 sq miles): at its longest point it stretches only 62km (39 miles) and at its widest a mere 48km (30 miles). The island lies 20° south of the equator, just within the southern boundary of the tropics.

Mauritius has two physical regions: a belt of coastal lowlands which skirts the island's perimeter and which varies in width – from a little under 2.5km (1.5 miles) in the south to 15km (9 miles) in the north – and a central plateau that rises, almost imperceptibly, to a height of between 350 and 700m (1000–2000ft). The profile of the plateau is more or less wedge-shaped, with the Savanne mountains in the south forming the highest point and the coastal lowlands in the north being the lowest-lying areas. Angular and pointed mountains rise up dramatically from the rolling fields of sugar cane (once dense tropical forests) that cover much of Mauritius: these are the remains of the volcano's ancient walls which Nature has not yet been successful in eroding away.

An almost continuous barrier of coral reefs virtually encircles the island with the only extensive gap being in the south, between Souillac and just to the north of Le Souffleur, where some of the island's major rivers discharge into the sea.

Also along this stretch of the Mauritian coastline the land gives way to the sea in a series of cliffs and steep slopes which drop away rapidly to great depths; thus there is no marked continental shelf which could be enclosed by a coral reef to continue the chain of turquoise

Left: *Windsurfing in the crystal-clear waters of Flic en Flac is a popular watersport.* Above: *The emblem of the Mauritius Marine Conservation Society is based on the balloon fish, and their newsletter* DIODON *is named after it.*

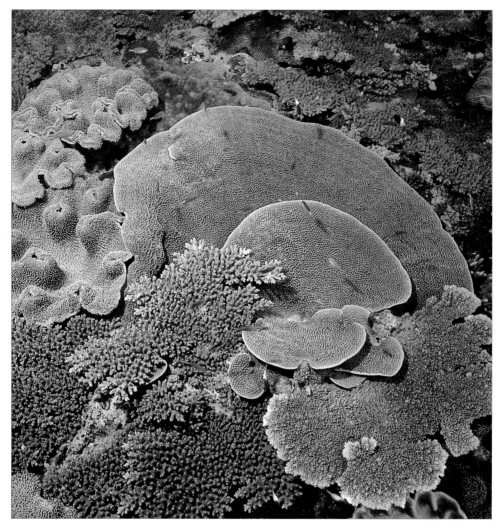

.Plate coral is aptly named for its appearance.

lagoons that surround the rest of the island. It is in these lagoons that snorkelling is the main form of diving, while scuba diving takes place on the coral-encrusted reefs and drop-offs that lie beyond.

CLIMATE

Mauritius has a tropical maritime climate that basically has only two seasons – summer and winter. The relative difference between these two seasons is so small that the intermediate seasons of spring and autumn are effectively smudged out. During the summer months (November to April), temperatures can climb as high as 35°C (95°F) on occasion, and, combined with high humidity levels, can become uncomfortable for people who are accustomed to a more temperate climate. During this summer period short, heavy bursts of rain cool the island, but there is a sting in the tail: when the sun comes out again the moisture left behind soon results in further humidity! The months of May to October are considered to be the island's winter period. During these months temperatures average a comfortable 25°C (77°F), humidity levels are reduced and the nights are cooler. An important element that helps to make the hot summer months reasonable are the southeast trade winds which bring cool air in from the sea, effectively fanning the island. In winter, however, these winds can become tiresome, particularly along the south and east coasts.

Lying within the tropics, as it does, means that Mauritius is subject to periodic attacks by tropical cyclones, also known as hurricanes and typhoons. When the right conditions prevail, enormous tropical depressions are created over the Indian Ocean some distance to the northeast of the island, and the resulting flow of air to fill these depressions can gust at speeds of up to 160kph (100mph). These swirling masses of air meander aimlessly across the ocean, causing little trouble until their path is interrupted by land, and then the fury of the cyclone is unleashed, rendering it capable of frenzied and ruthless destruction.

Generally, Mauritius is only subjected to this punishment on a large scale once every 15 years or so, although cyclones of lesser magnitude occur virtually every year.

The people of the island are well prepared for the onslaught. With modern technology the likely path of an approaching cyclone can be tracked and its estimated time of arrival calculated fairly accurately, allowing Mauritians time to batten down.

Most of the island's buildings are designed and built to accommodate the full force of Nature's might, and destruction is thus minimized. Food stocks are laid in and water reserves are built up while the winds do their war dance prior to attack.

The onslaught is swift and its course unpredictable as the winds veer from side to side, searching for chinks in the island's armour; and then, after what seems like an eternity, there is calm whilst the eye of the storm surveys the damage done. An eerie lull settles over the island as people slowly lift their heads to take stock, knowing that the distant roar is the other half of Nature's army clamouring to descend upon them with all its tempestuous weapons of war.

Fortunately, however, the little island of Mauritius is often bypassed by the frequent cyclones that the Indian Ocean generates annually. Occasionally it may be lashed by violent rainstorms and heavy winds created by a cyclone that may come close. But this often helps to clear the air and cool the island down after a spell of hot, humid weather.

The island's undulating topography, together with its differences in altitude, its variable winds and the influence of the surrounding sea, combine to create varied microclimates, the result being that it may be raining on the plateau at Curepipe, and at the same time be hot and dry on the beach. Due to the effects of altitude and the cooling influence of the wind there is an approximate temperature difference of 5°C (41°F) between the cool highlands and the warm coast. Notwithstanding the occasional storm and heavy winds, Mauritius has a good climate all year round for visitors who want to have fun in the sun, and seasonal differences are so small that there really is no 'good' or 'bad' time to be there. Having said that, there could be a slight preference for the months of October and November – particularly for divers – because they are usually the driest months and fall outside the normal cyclone season when the winds can be a problem.

NATURAL VEGETATION

Mauritius was once densely covered by hardwood forest and lush vegetation. The trees that made up this woodland were tall and straight and therefore sought after by early settlers for export to Europe where they were turned into timber for ship-building, the construction of houses and furniture. The island was further cleared of its natural forest and bush in order to make way for large sugar-cane fields which were planted in more and more areas after the

French arrived in 1715. Today, the only remaining natural forests are hidden away in rugged valleys or on steep mountain slopes. The few patches of natural woodland found on open ground are legally protected by high fences against the further encroachment of man.

The island is well endowed with a blaze of colourful flowers. There is bougainvillea with its coat of many colours, yellow alamanda flowers, the flaming red frangipani trees, hibiscus, strelitzia, anthuriums, orchids, oleanders and poinsettias, all of which grow prolifically. Nature has done much to try to hide the scars of the past and the human intrusion of today.

BIRDLIFE

Mauritius does not have either the quantity or the variety of birdlife that other islands in the Indian Ocean have – notably the Seychelles. Indeed when the island was covered in verdant mountain forests and man had not yet set foot upon its soil, there were only some 26 species which inhabited Mauritius. Perhaps the best known indigenous bird was the dodo (*Raphus cucullatus*), a flightless bird that became extinct less than 100 years after the first explorers landed on the island and in so doing gave rise to the well-known term used to indicate extinction: 'as dead as a dodo'.

Notwithstanding the relative ornithological paucity, the island is nevertheless home to a number of important bird species, such as the Echo Parakeet, the world's rarest, and the highly endangered Mauritius Kestrel. Other birds endemic to Mauritius and, sadly, all threatened species in one way or another are the Pink Pigeon, the Mauritius Cuckoo-shrike, the Mauritius Black Bulbul, the Mascarene Paradise Flycatcher, the Mauritius Fody and the Mauritius Olive White-eye.

ANIMALS

The fact that Mauritius is a remote and small volcanic island in the middle of a vast ocean allowed no opportunity for the migration of animals to the island from the cradles of their creation on the African and Asian continents. In fact, the only mammals indigenous to Mauritius were two species of fruit bats (one of which is now extinct) and three species of insectivorous bats. As a result the ancestors of all the animals which are now living on the island today were brought there by settlers. The Dutch brought Tundjuc deer from Java and pigs from Holland. The Portuguese introduced the Macaque monkey in 1528 which they brought from Malaysia, and the tenrec, an insectivorous creature resembling a hedgehog, was introduced from Madagascar. The ancestors of the giant tortoises that can be seen today at the Sir Seewoosagur Ramgoolam Botanical Gardens and at the Casela Bird Park were re-introduced to the island from Aldabra in 1875. The hump-backed Zebu cattle, occasionally seen pulling carts along the island's crowded roads, were introduced from Madagascar.

THE PEOPLE – A BRIEF HISTORY

The first recorded sighting of Mauritius was made in the 10th century by Arab mariners. They called the island Dina Harobi – Arabic for 'abandoned island'. Mauritian historians believe that they probably gave the island this name because they came upon it shortly after it had been struck by a cyclone, and the island looked devastated and abandoned. The Arabs did not stay and they left no trace of their visit other than on their rough maps, where they briefly mentioned the volcanic island sighted on their voyages south. The next record of its existence was made some 500 years later when Portuguese explorer Diego Fernandez Pereira came upon the island in 1507. He named it Isla do Cerne (Swan Island). There are two schools of thought as to why he gave the island that name; some people say he associated the dodos with swans, and others that he named it after his ship, *Cerne*.

Most of Mauritius's terrestrial animal life was introduced to the island by settlers, as was the Javanese deer.

In or around 1528 another Portuguese explorer, Don Diego Rodriquez rediscovered the island of Rodrigues, which was named after him and lies some 560km (348 miles) east of Mauritius. He named the archipelago of Isla do Cerne (Mauritius), the present-day Réunion and Rodrigues the 'Mascarenes' after the Portuguese admiral Don Pedro Mascarenhas.

From time to time the Portuguese used Isla do Cerne as a halfway station to India, in order to take on fresh water and food supplies. They also used it as a place of refuge when the weather turned foul. But they did not colonize the island. This was left to the Dutch who, in 1598 under the command of Vice Admiral Wybrandt van Warwyck of the Dutch East India Company, anchored off the beaches at a place later called Vieux Grand Port, which is situated in Grand Port Bay in the southeast corner of the island. He named the bay Warwyck Bay and called the island Mauritius, after Prince Maurice of Orange and Nassau, the Stadtholder of Holland. The Dutch found Mauritius to be conveniently situated in relation to their trade with both India and Batavia (Java) and so they set about establishing a base on the island. However, they too had no intention of colonizing it; they merely wanted to use it as a victualling station and to exploit its rich timber resources. But they abandoned Mauritius in 1658, after being there for some 60 years, because it became unnecessary to have a base on the island as well as at the Cape of Good Hope, where a station had been established some six years previously. In 1663 the Dutch East India Company, regretting its decision to withdraw from Mauritius, decided to repossess it. They established a small base in the south and built a fort at Noordt Wester Haven (Port Louis) in order to prevent the island from falling into the hands of the English or French. This garrison remained there until 1710 when the Dutch withdrew from the island and the last governor, Abraham Momber van de Velde, left Mauritius and set sail for Batavia on the *Beverwaart*.

In 1715 Captain Dufresne d'Arsel of the French East India Company took possession of the island in the name of his king and named it Ile de France in his honour. The French decided to colonize the island and some seven years later the first settlers arrived to establish a permanent home there. The French moved their base from Port Bourbon, the name d'Arsel had given to Warwyck Bay, and established a new one at Noordt Wester Haven which they called Port Louis. This move was made because of the better protection afforded to ships anchored there, the easier approaches to the harbour and the less windy conditions that prevail on that part of the island.

In 1735 the French East India Company appointed an energetic and highly competent administrator, Bertrand François Mahé de Labourdonnais, to governorship of the island. The brief from his employers dictated that he was to dig French roots deep into the soils of the island and this he did with enthusiasm and vigour. Among the many things he did was to institute a town-planning scheme for Port Louis; he cleaned up its environs which had been badly neglected and he improved the island's administrative structure and systems. He bought Mon Plaisir, an estate situated just north of Port Louis, on which he established a vegetable garden and a nursery to cultivate spices and other plants with commercial value which were suitable for Mauritian soils. He promoted the increased production of sugar cane and imported the first sugar mill for his farm Villebague. Under his leadership, order and purpose were established on the island and Ile de France began to prosper.

Port Louis became an important base from which the French could penetrate the hitherto unexplored areas of the Indian Ocean and from which they could operate against English shipping bound to and from India. This was very significant, particularly during the Seven Years' War (1756–1763) when competition in international trade between the two protagonists became deadly. Corsairs were also encouraged to establish bases at Port Louis, and in exchange for payment to the Governor were promised both security and safety. When Napoleon held sway over France he consolidated the French hold over the island by sending General Charles Decaen to ensure total obedience to the French emperor. This was necessary in the light of growing hostility between France and England and the increasing importance of trade with India. But, as more and more ships flying the royal ensign fell into the hands of French corsairs, who quickly scuttled back to the safety of Port Louis when challenged, the British need to take over the island increased.

Eventually in 1810 the die was cast and a British squadron of four ships sailed into Grand Port Bay and engaged a French flotilla of four ships (later reinforced by three more from Port Louis), in a fierce battle that lasted for nearly three days. Eventually the British were forced to admit defeat – their only naval trouncing in the Napoleonic era.

But the ire of Albion had been raised and the English returned some six months later with an armada of 20 war ships, backed by a sizable fleet of transport and support ships and an army of 12,000 men. This time they anchored beyond the reef at Cap Malheureux in the very north of the island and the army was conveyed ashore in small boats through a tiny gap in the reef. The men landed without incident and marched on Port Louis. Attempts, brave but futile, were made to stop the advancing army at Grand Bay, Arsenal Bay and Baie du Tombeau. But four days after landing, General Decaen surrendered to General Abercrombie and Ile de France became part of the British empire.

At the Treaty of Paris in 1814, Ile de France, Rodrigues and Seychelles were confirmed as British dependencies and once again the island's name changed – this time back to Mauritius. The British did not want to colonize the island; indeed they had no desire to change its character in any way – they merely wanted to ensure that Mauritius would never again become a threat to their shipping. Franco-Mauritians were allowed to retain their language, religion and sugar estates; the Napoleonic legal system was endorsed and Robert Farquhar, the first British governor, recognized the French civil administration system. For the next 150 or more years – until independence in 1968 – an amicable balance was achieved between British political control and civil administration, and Franco-Mauritian economic control and way of life.

In 1835 slavery was abolished, but as the Mauritian sugar industry continued to expand during the 19th century, so the demand for labour grew. Because of England's connection with India the importation of indentured labour from that continent began in earnest. The island's human population began to swell rapidly after this period as indentured labourers and their families became permanent settlers. By 1865 immigrants from India and their descendants constituted the largest racial group in Mauritius.

In 1936 the Mauritian Labour Party was formed to fight for the rights of labourers on the sugar estates. In the 1950s the party was led by the indomitable fighter for worker rights, Dr (later Sir) Seewoosagur Ramgoolam, who left an indelible mark on the pages of Mauritian

Eureka, one of the original estate homes found on the sugar plantations, is now an art gallery and museum.

A Tamil-speaking Hindu during the Cavadee *festival.*

history and whose name is honoured by the many places, institutions and buildings that are named after him. In 1948 the first step towards a democratic government was taken when the franchise was extended to adults over 21 who could write their name. In 1959 the franchise was opened to all adults and a Hindu majority was guaranteed at the polls. Discord developed between the Travaillistes, supporters of the Labour Party which campaigned for political independence from Britain, and supporters of Parti Mauricien Social Democrate (PMSD), who were predominantly Creole (and Franco-Mauritian) and who did not want independence. Riots broke out on the streets of Port Louis and tension mounted as the day of political independence drew closer. The British sent troops to restore law and order and to keep the peace.

On 12 March 1968 Mauritius became an independent member of the Commonwealth. Dr Seewoosagur Ramgoolam was elected the first prime minister and a coalition of the major political parties was in power.

Since then the country has had its fair share of internal political disagreement and dissension, but differences have been fought in parliament and resolution has been sought through the ballot box. In 1992 Mauritius became a Republic and Sir Anerood Jugnauth was elected the country's first president.

The wheels of industry turned very slowly after independence, particularly as attempts were made to diversify the economy and so reduce its dependence on its single crop – sugar. But steadily the engines of growth have gathered momentum and the wheels are turning considerably faster every year. A successful programme encouraging export-orientated industries to Mauritius has been achieved through the establishment of a dedicated Export Processing Zone, with an attendant package of incentives, in a specialized industrial area situated between Port Louis and Curepipe.

Tourism has been encouraged and has expanded from an industry which had only two or three beach hotels and one acceptable commercial hotel in the early 1970s to one which has 85 registered hotels today, many of which are resort hotels of the highest standing and can compete favourably with the best in the world. Visitors to the island have increased from some 18,000 in 1970 to over 400,000 in 1994 and income from tourism has risen from Rs18 million to Rs6 billion over the same period.

The Mauritian government is fully committed to the free enterprise economic system and it has made great strides in building up a healthy economy. Indeed amongst many international experts the country is held up as a model for the economic restructuring and transformation of a developing country.

THE PEOPLE TODAY – A HUMAN POTPOURRI

Mauritius was, until relatively recently, an uninhabited island without a history of human habitation. The ancestors of its present-day inhabitants therefore come from other lands, and they have brought with them memories and traditions relating to the countries from whence they came. There are Franco-Mauritians whose forebears came from France and who were the first to settle permanently on the island. They brought the French language, customs and legal system, and implanted a character in the island that is unmistakably French. Then there are inhabitants who came from Africa and Madagascar as slaves to work on the sugar estates. From these people has evolved the Creole population which constitutes the second largest racial component of Mauritian society. The Creoles brought a vibrancy, an innate charm and the rhythm of Africa to the Mauritian cultural melting pot. They also took the French language and gave it a Mauritian flavour and the result – Creole – has become the lingua franca of the island. There are people who were indentured in India to work on the sugar plantations, but have stayed to become leaders, businesspeople and professionals, and now form the majority of the island's population. They brought with them Indian religions and customs that have become important constituents of the Mauritian character. In 1826 Chinese labourers were recruited to work on the sugar estates and they, too, stayed. With them has come the inscrutability and politeness of the Orient, as well as the fascination of a Chinatown in Port Louis and the fun of Chinese New Year celebrations.

Each racial group has added its own fragrance to the Mauritian potpourri and the blend that has emerged is refreshing. It provides an example to the world of how people from different backgrounds, different cultures, different language groups and who worship different gods, can come together to form a single nation.

Sega dancing is a very popular sensuous, rhythmic Creole tradition.

TRAVELLING TO AND IN MAURITIUS

Getting There

If you do not intend to sail to Mauritius on a yacht or to visit the island from a cruise ship, the easiest and quickest way to get there is by air. The island is well served by a number of international airlines. Air Mauritius, the national carrier, offers a regular service to and from various destinations in Europe, Africa, Asia and the Indian Ocean islands' airports, including London, Paris, Amsterdam, Rome, Munich, Frankfurt, Zürich, Geneva, Nairobi, Johannesburg, Cape Town, Durban, Harare, Bombay, Singapore, Hong Kong, Kuala Lumpur, Moroni, Madagascar, Réunion and Rodrigues.

The island is served by most international airlines, including South African Airways, British Airways, Lufthansa, Air France, Air India, Air Madagascar, Singapore Airlines, Air Tanzania, Air Zimbabwe and Air Zambia. Mauritius has only one international airport, the Sir Seewoosagur Ramgoolam International Airport at Plaisance.

Flight information can be obtained from individual airlines or from any of the Air Mauritius offices around the globe.

TELEPHONE DIALLING CODE
Should you wish to make hotel and other reservations on the island in advance, the area code for Mauritius is (230).

VISA AND HEALTH REQUIREMENTS
There are no special visa requirements for Mauritius. Should you plan to extend your visit to Réunion, then necessary visa requirements are as for France. Yellow fever vaccination and related documentation is required if you arrive from an infected area.

Left: *The luxurious Touessrok Hotel, situated along the water's edge, is joined to the mainland by a wooden footbridge.* Above: *A Yellow-edged moray eel peers out of its hiding place in a coral reef.*

Getting Around the Island

By Air
Air Mauritius offers a chartered helicopter service which operates out of Sir Seewoosagur Ramgolam (SSR) International Airport at Plaisance.

Air transfers between the airport and all leading hotels around the island can be arranged. The helicopter is available for other charter work as well.

By Bus
Buses in Mauritius are plentiful and the service is frequent, except after 17:30. There are two bus stations in Port Louis, one serving the north and the other serving the plateau towns of Beau Bassin, Rose Hill, Quatre Bornes and Curepipe in the south. Don't be put off by the appearance of some of the buses – they still get there! Bus stops are distinguished by their white lettering on a black background. Tickets are purchased from the bus conductors (most of whom don't wear a uniform) – make sure you keep your ticket as they do regular checks.

A train service is no longer available in Mauritius: it was dispensed with shortly after World War II.

By Taxi
Generally speaking, taxis are bad news on the island. Many are in poor condition and a good number do not have meters (and if they do, they are seldom used), so it is advisable to negotiate your fare with the taxi-driver before you get in. Taxis are easily identified by their number plates – black lettering on white plates.

Fares are expensive and so taxis should be avoided other than for short distances within Port Louis and the major towns. A round trip is normally negotiated whereby the driver holds you responsible for his return fare to the starting point – even if you don't wish to make a return trip. For longer journeys it may pay you to negotiate a fee for hiring a taxi for the whole day rather than hiring a car and driving yourself.

By Bike
Hiring a bicycle, a facility offered by most hotels, pensions and guesthouses, is a wonderful way of seeing the island, but can be more than a little scary on some of the busy roads, so choose your routes carefully. Distances between towns are not great and there are beautiful views of the island around every corner. One is, of course, never far from a beach and relaxation.

By Boat
A wonderful way to see the island is by boat – indeed some people say it is the most picturesque way of seeing Mauritius. Yachts can be chartered in Grand Baie, and most hotels in the north and northwest of the island can arrange for boats trips around Ile Plate (Flat Island), Coin de Mire (Gunner's Quoin) and down to Baie du Tombeau (Bay of Tombs), where the *Isla Mauritia*, a yacht that was built in 1852 and which is, incredibly, still used for charters around the island, can be seen.

Car Hire
Bookings can be made on arrival at SSR International Airport, or, alternately, at the reception of your hotel. Competition between the various operators is keen and it is, therefore, advisable to shop around before hiring a vehicle. It is also possible to negotiate deals with private car owners, but this can be a risky business.

An international driver's licence is not required, but it is necessary for the hirer to be over 23 years of age and in possession of a valid licence from his or her home country.

MAJOR CAR-HIRE COMPANIES

The major car-hire companies operating in Mauritius are:

ABC Motors Co. Ltd.	Port Louis Cnr Abattoir & Military Roads	Tel: 242-1177 Fax: 242-1193
Avis	Port Louis Al-Madina Street	Tel: 208-1624 Fax: 208-1014
Beach Car Ltd.	Grand Baie Royal Road	Tel: 263-8759
Budget Car Hire	Grand Gaube Main Road	Tel: 263-8937
Dodo Touring	Quatre Bornes St Jean Road	Tel: 425-6810
Europcar	Autorente M2 Pailles	Tel: 208-9258 Fax: 208-4705
	Grand Baie SSR Airport	Tel: 263-7948 Tel: 637-3240
Fone-A-Car Ltd.	Vacoas 20 Thompson Street	Tel: 686-5502
Grand Bay Top Tours Ltd.	Grand Baie Royal Road	Tel: 263-8770
Hertz Maurtourco	Curepipe Curepipe Road	Tel: 674-3695 Fax 674-3720
Kevtrav	Quatre Bornes 6 Orchidées Avenue	Tel: 454-5760
Maurent	Port Louis 5 Madagascar Street	Tel: 212-2080 Fax: 212-2078
Société JHA Araulphy & Cie.	Mahébourg Labourdonnais Street	Tel: 631-9806 Fax: 631-9991
Waterlily Travel and Tours	Curepipe 15 Malartic Street	Tel: 676-1496

A typical beach scene on the island – lazy, languid, sunshine-filled days in idyllic surroundings.

MAJOR TOUR OPERATORS

The major tour operators in Mauritius are:

Concorde Travel & Tours Port Louis Tel: 208-5041
La Chaussée Fax: 212-2585

Hertz Maurtourco Curepipe Tel: 675-1453
Fraserville Lane Fax: 675-6425

Mauritius Travel & Tourism Bureau Floréal Tel: 696-3001
Royal Road Fax: 696-3012

Mauritours and Vacances Evasion Rose Hill Tel: 454-1666
5 Venkatasananda Street Fax: 454-1682

White Sand Tours Port Louis Tel: 212-3712
IBL Tourism Division Fax: 208-8524
Al-Madina Street
Motorway A1

CURRENCY OF THE ISLAND

The currency is the Mauritian rupee (Rs), which is divided into 100 cents. Since February 1983, the rupee has been pegged to a basket of currencies with a view to minimizing fluctuations in the exchange rate of the rupee.

Mauritius has a well-developed banking system, with no less than 13 commercial banks, many of whom have branches throughout the country.

LANGUAGES

Although English is the official language of the island, most people speak French and/or Creole in Mauritius. Indeed, English is seldom heard beyond the corridors of business and the bureaucracy.

Creole is a French patois and is the lingua franca of the island. Virtually every Mauritian can speak the language and it is the mother tongue of the island's majority. Although the language is used in many social contexts it tends to have a low status, probably due to its largely slave origin. Most of the island's newspapers are written in French, and it is the language used on television and radio.

Hindi is widely spoken by many of the island's Hindus and about 10 percent of the population consider Hindi to be their home language.

Although Telugu, Tamil, Gujerati and Marathi are also heard on the island, only Tamil is spoken to any extent.

DIVING AND SNORKELLING IN MAURITIUS

Comparisons are always odious, but unfortunately we are all guilty of making them. Mauritius is frequently compared with other diving areas in the Indian Ocean, such as the Seychelles, the Maldives and the Kenyan coastline, and even with the Red Sea. Usually Mauritius comes off badly – simply because people expect the same conditions and underwater scenery as can be found in these diving areas.

Of course Mauritius is none of these. The result is that the idea of diving in Mauritius may then be tossed to one side with a disparaging remark and the opportunity to enjoy a magnificent underwater experience is lost: the island has some amazing diving experiences to offer, such as playing with Eagle-rays, watching sharks hunt their prey, swimming through forests of gorgonia – some over 2m (6.6ft) in height, seeing walking fish flex their beautiful butterfly wings when they feel threatened, passing through lobster-filled chimneys and canyons, feeling the power and purpose of tuna, wahoo and even marlin as they propel their way through your dive site, observing the quiet diffidence of shoals of kingfish that briefly encircle you and then move off, leaving you wondering whether their suspicions were satisfied. Each is a unique experience that makes diving in Mauritius a different and pleasurable adventure. There are also many dive sites which are filled with tropical fish so that diving in these areas is like diving in an open aquarium. Mauritius has all this, but it also has something more: some of the most relaxed, amiable and professionally operated diving centres in the world. Here you are not a number, or just another diver waiting in a queue to be whisked off to a dive site and taken down by a divemaster who has become an automaton, then dropped back at the dive centre while impatient staff push for your gear so that they can keep their diving machine in motion. In Mauritius the natural hospitality of the people comes bubbling through and you are soon made to feel as if you are diving with 'buddies' whom you have known all your life.

Left: *The tropical waters of the Indian Ocean harbour many gems of great beauty.* Above: *This Moorish idol, an aquarium fish, has several rows of brush-like teeth.*

Dive centres are usually based at major hotels on the island.

There are currently 23 diving centres in Mauritius that are registered with the Mauritius Scuba Diving Association (MSDA). Each centre is run by a professional who conspicuously enjoys what he is doing, making diving in Mauritius a friendly and satisfying experience. All the divemasters are multilingual, so language is seldom an obstacle. But even if it is, the innate geniality of the Mauritian people soon overcomes it. Diving in Mauritius should be viewed as an enjoyable part of an overall holiday experience, rather than as the sole motivation for going to Mauritius.

The nature of Mauritian diving is based on the topography of the country's coastline, which in typical cross section looks like this:

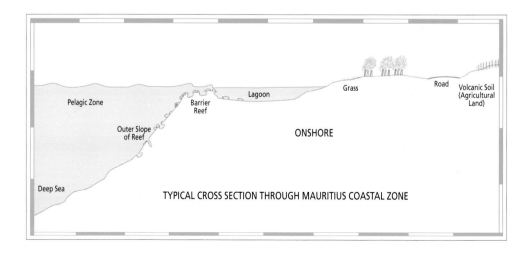

Snorkelling is done within the lagoons created by the barrier reef, while scuba diving is done on the continental shelf and down the drop-off that lies beyond. Since the barrier reef almost entirely encircles Mauritius, creating the tranquil lagoons which surround the island, there are vast areas where it is possible to snorkel. As a general rule the closer the diver gets to the encircling reef the more exciting and colourful the coral and fish life becomes. However, for the purposes of this book and because it is possible to snorkel in most of the water surrounding the island, we have concentrated on scuba diving sites except where the snorkelling opportunities are exceptional.

There are three levels or types of scuba diving available on the island. The first is learner diving which can be done with any one of the 23 MSDA-affiliated diving centres operating in Mauritius. With one or two exceptions each of the dive centres offers training to beginners – from an introductory course through to a one-star certificate, which is an internationally accepted qualification entitling the recipient to dive anywhere in the world, subject to certain conditions. Each of the dive centres is affiliated to one or more of the international diving associations (the most common ones are listed on page 36) and so training and diving standards are strictly maintained and regulated accordingly.

The second level applies to qualified divers who are in possession of a valid diving certificate and an updated logbook. The dive centres in Mauritius normally operate a

TAKING THE PLUNGE

With the increase in popularity of scuba diving, operators offering training courses at what seem to be bargain prices have suddenly emerged.

Before you sign up for a course, be sure to ask a few basic questions. Sensible queries include:

What training materials are available?
A five-star centre affiliated to any of the international diving associations (PADI, MSDA, CMSA, DIWA) should include training manuals, slides and videos in its courses.

How many instructors will teach the course?
It is best to stick with a single instructor throughout the course so that a good degree of trust can be built up between students and instructor.

What is the maximum number of students allowed on a course?
As a guide, the maximum number of students allocated to a single instructor on an open-water course is eight, although this may be increased to 10 if a certified assistant is employed.

Once a course has started, will more students be allowed to join?
When this happens it causes problems for everyone. If you're already on the course there is little you can do. However, if you discover that a dive centre permits this, rather train elsewhere.

What is included in the cost?
Watch out for hidden extras, such as equipment hire, which should normally be included in the course fee. Also, check that the fee includes the training manual, any boat trips to and from the dive site, and the certification.

six-day week with a morning dive at 09:30 and an afternoon dive at 13:30 (depending on demand) and so it is possible for suitably qualified divers to arrange a dive at a time and place of their choice. The most popular dive sites in each subregion of Mauritius and the dive centres operating in these subregions are described in the Regional Directories at the end of each Dive Sites section (pages 40–114). Most dives in this category are at depths varying from 10–30m (33–99ft).

The third level of diving applies to visitors who want to dive 'off the beaten track'. Invariably this means deep diving, down to 60m (197ft), as well as more hazardous diving in terms of currents, the presence of sharks and so on. Obviously only experienced and well-qualified divers are considered for this level of diving, and divemasters will insist on taking divers who are unknown to them on a number of familiarization dives first. But the rewards

Glowfish, Soldierfish and Goatfish abound at Coral Gardens.

for the more adventurous divers are substantial as another, infinitely exciting, diving world opens up at this challenging level. There are three particular dive centres which offer specialist diving in Mauritius on a regular basis and arrangements should be made with one of the following:

Villas Caroline Diving Centre	Flic en Flac	Tel: 453-8450
	Contact: Mr Pierre Szalay	Fax: 453-8144
Blue Water Diving Centre	Le Corsaire, Trou aux Biches	Tel: 261-5209
	Contact: Mr Hugues Vitry	Fax: 261-6267
Sindbad Ltd.	Kux Village, Cap Malheureux	Tel: 415-1518
	Contact: Mr Uwe Ertl	Fax: 262-7407

With the exception of the above, most of the remaining dive centres are hotel-based and, therefore, localized in their operation – each centre primarily serves the guests of the hotel in which it is based (although without exception outsiders are also welcome).

The dive sites are shared by all the dive centres operating in the subregion. However, individual dive centres may have additional sites known only to them, and they may also tackle common dive sites differently – for example, dividing one area into different dives, or starting on a drop-off at the deepest part of the dive and then ascending to the shallowest, or doing the dive in the reverse direction.

In view of the marked regionalism in the development of tourist facilities on the island, diving centres and therefore diving in Mauritius is also regionalized.

The following diving subregions have been identified:

SOUTHWEST

Easydive Diving Centre	Berjaya Hotel, Le Morne Contact: Emanuele Senatore	Tel: 638-6800 Fax: 683-6070
Diveplan Ltd.	Le Brabant Hotel Contact: Mike Frédéric	Tel: 683-6775 Fax: 683-6786
Odyssee Diving Centre	Centre du Pêche, Black River Contact: Jacques Angélique	Tel: 683-6503 Fax: 683-6318

WEST (all in Flic en Flac)

Sofitel Diving Centre	Le Sofitel Imperial Hotel Contact: Nasser A. Beeharry	Tel: 453-8700 Fax: 453-8320
La Pirogue Diving Centre	La Pirogue Hotel Contact: Thierry de Chazal	Tel: 453-8441 Fax: 453-8449
Villas Caroline Diving Centre	Villas Caroline Beach Hotel Contact: Pierre Szalay	Tel: 453-8450 Fax: 453-8144
Klondike Diving Centre	Le Klondike Hotel Contact: Jean Phillipe Appadoo	Tel: 453-8335 Fax: 453-8337

NORTHWEST

Turtle Bay Nautics	Maritim Hotel, Balaclava Contact: Denis Vitry	Tel: 261-5600 Fax: 261-5670
Nautilus Diving Centre	Trou aux Biches Village Hotel Contact: Raymond Lai-Cheong	Tel: 261-6562 Fax: 261-6611
Blue Water Diving Centre	Le Corsaire Angling Centre Contact: Hugues Vitry	Tel: 261-5209 Fax: 261-6267
Paradise Diving Centre	PLM Mont Choisy Hotel Contact: Kevin Cock	Tel: 263-7220 Fax: 263-8534

NORTH

Diving World	Le Mauricia Hotel, Grand Baie Contact: Michael Dufour	Tel: 263-7800 Fax: 263-7888
Islandive Ltd.	Veranda Bungalow Villas Contact: Geni and Pappy Bordie	Tel: 263-8016 Fax: 263-7369
Merville Diving Centre	Merville Hotel, Grand Baie Contact: Tim Lai Cheong	Tel: 263-8621 Fax: 263-8146
Dolphin Diving Centre	Royal Road, Grand Baie Contact: Gowtan Garroby	Tel: 263-7273
Sindbad Ltd.	Kux Village, Cap Malheureux Contact: Uwe Ertl	Tel: 262-8836 Fax:262-7407
The Cap Divers Ltd.	Le Paradise Cove, Anse La Raie Contact: Marie-Christine and Karl Heinz Berger	Tel: 262-7983 Fax: 262-7736

EAST

The Cap Divers Ltd.	Belle Mare Plage Hotel, Belle Mare Contact: Marie-Christine Berger	Tel: 416-1518 Fax 415-1993
Explorer Diving Centre	Hotel Ambre, Belle Mare, Palmar Contact: Ben & Yannick Cadet	Tel: 415-1544 Fax: 415-1594
St Géran Diving Centre	Le St Géran Hotel, Poste de Flacq Contact: Alain Randiame	Tel: 415-1825 Fax: 415-1983
Pierre Sport Diving	Le Touessrok Hotel, Trou d'Eau Douce Contact: Anthony Pierre	Tel: 419-2451 Fax: 419-2025

SOUTH

Coral Dive Centre	La Croix du Sud Hotel, Pointe Jerome, Mahébourg Contact: Henri Autard	Tel: 631-9505 Fax: 631-9603
Shandrani Diving Centre	Shandrani Hotel, Blue Bay Contact: Dirk Olivier	Tel: 637-3511 Fax: 637-4313

The devil firefish is well camouflaged in the coral alongside a needle sea urchin. Both are dangerous to handle.

Diving and Snorkelling Equipment

Although you can hire diving equipment throughout the island, it is preferable to have your own. Apart from the fact that you save money in the long term, rented equipment can sometimes be unsuitable. There is nothing worse than a mask that leaks …

MASKS

Make sure the mask you choose fits properly. Most masks now have frames made from pure silicone; these are more pleasant to wear and they last longer. The mask should form a good seal against your face and should feel comfortable. To check for the correct fit, first fold the strap over the faceplate, so that it is out of the way, and press the mask onto your face while looking at the ceiling. Then breathe in through your nose and look downwards. The mask should stay firmly on your face as long as you continue to inhale. Roll your eyes from left to right and up and down to make sure your field of vision is good.

SNORKELS

Snorkels are not only used by snorkellers: divers always carry one in order to save air supplies while at the surface or in case of a long swim back to the boat or shore. A good snorkel allows you to breathe comfortably while cruising on the surface with your face in the water. Ideally your snorkel should have a short, wide barrel; these are easier to breathe through than long, thin barrels. The mouthpiece should be soft and pliable, and should feel comfortable in your mouth. Many snorkels now have swivelling mouthpieces, or mouthpieces that mould themselves to your mouth-shape for greater comfort. You can also obtain snorkels that have built-in self-draining valves at the base of the tube, so that the snorkel is

Divers doing their mandatory decompression stop before the final ascent to the surface.

automatically cleared of water when you surface. These valves have become much more reliable in recent years, even though some consider them unnecessary. The snorkel can be kept in position by slipping it under the mask strap. Alternatively, you can use a snorkel-keeper – a retaining ring, available with a quick-release device, that attaches to the strap. Whatever you choose, always carry a spare mask strap with you in case the one that you are using breaks.

FINS

Fins provide fast and easy propulsion through the water. There are two types:

• **Full-foot fins** have a built-in foot pocket, so that your foot is embraced from your toes to your heel. They are usually smaller and less powerful than the more widely used open-heel fins.

• **Open-heel fins** only cover the front part of your foot, and are usually worn with bootees; an adjustable strap goes around the back of your heel and helps to keep the fin comfortably in place.

This combination of bootee and fin has considerable advantages over the full-foot system; for example, you can walk on land wearing just the bootees and then put the fins on once you're in the water.

The blades of the fins are usually made from a combination of rubber and plastic. Some have ribs down the side to improve swimming efficiency; the ribs channel the water and prevent the blade from twisting. Others have vents to reduce the effort of the recovery kick. As with masks, it is a good idea to carry a spare fin strap.

OTHER DIVE GEAR

• Many divers prefer to carry their own regulator and depth gauge. If you coil this assemblage around your other belongings it doesn't take up much room in your luggage. Carrying your own equipment, if you are confident of its reliability, makes you far more relaxed about a dive, as long as you follow your dive plan.
• All dive centres in Mauritius hire out the full range of diving equipment required, including wetsuits, tanks, fins and snorkelling gear, but you may wish to take much of your own equipment with you. If you do, a dive computer, an underwater torch (necessary for night dives), and a knife should be at the top of your list.

RECOMPRESSION (HYPERBARIC) CHAMBERS

There is only one facility on the island, situated at the paramilitary Special Mobile Force at Vacoas, and it is important that you make a note of the emergency number before diving.

Learning to Dive

Anyone who is reasonably fit can learn to dive, and there is no better place to do it than in the tropics, where the waters are warm and where, of course, the beauty of the underwater world is likely to make you wonder why it took you so long to try it. There are plenty of dive centres in Mauritius that offer training courses.

It is perfectly feasible to walk up to a beach-front dive-shop in nothing but your swimsuit and join up for a diving course: everything you need can be supplied. Many people do, however, prefer to buy their own basic kit – mask, snorkel and fins – which they can take anywhere with them. A wetsuit is another handy item to own as, although it is not a necessity in the warm waters of the tropics, a wetsuit can protect you from cuts and grazes and, more importantly, from the stings of marine organisms.

The main training agencies to look for are PADI (Professional Association of Diving Instructors), CMAS (World Underwater Federation), NAUI (National Association of Underwater Instructors), SSI (Scuba Schools International) and BSAC (British Sub-Aqua Club). In Mauritius most dive centres are affiliated to CMAS, but some also have affiliations to PADI, NAUI, DIWA and BSAC. Steer clear of two-tank operations working out of a beach shack. If someone approaches you on the beach and suggests you go diving, check their credentials. If the person is well qualified, fine; if not, don't go. If they are unhappy about your checking their credentials, assume the worst.

QUALIFICATIONS

Almost all dive centres in Mauritius offer a 'resort course'. This does not lead to a diving qualification but it does allow you to go underwater with an instructor to see whether or not you want to take up the sport in the longer term.

The main qualification to aim for at the start is an Open-Water One certificate. This usually involves five or six days of intensive training – classroom work (covering the theory and practice of diving, medical and safety procedures, etc.), pool work, some shallow dives – followed by a number of qualifying dives at sea.

Some agencies also offer what are known as 'referral courses'. These involve learning the basics in your home country – five classroom sessions, five pool sessions – and then completing your qualifying dives on arrival at your destination. The advantage of this system is that you need spend only the first two days of your holiday under instruction and are thereafter free to enjoy the rest of it diving.

Once you have passed your tests you will be issued with a 'C' card from one of the regulatory bodies. This is the diver's equivalent of a driving licence and permits you, anywhere in the world, to hire tanks and go diving – always, for safety reasons, with a companion (your 'buddy'). Your Open-Water Certification successfully acquired, you can train for higher qualifications: Advanced Open-Water, Rescue Diving, Divemaster and beyond. Alternatively, you might opt for special certifications such as Wreck Diver or Cave Diver.

HAZARDS

Diving is a relatively safe sport as long as the divers are thoroughly trained and follow the rules correctly. Never contemplate taking a diving course without having had a medical checkup, either before leaving home or on arrival in the country. Among conditions that preclude your taking up diving are epilepsy, heart disease, chest complaints, bronchitis, asthma and chronic ear and sinus problems. Don't deceive yourself into thinking 'it'll probably be all right'; it quite possibly won't be.

Training begins in a swimming pool, where divers familiarize themselves with equipment and techniques.

Flying after diving carries significant hazards. Once you have surfaced after a dive it takes several hours for the residual nitrogen in your body to disperse; were you to get straight into a plane, the low pressure inside the aircraft could cause this residual nitrogen to emerge as bubbles in your bloodstream, causing decompression sickness ('the bends'). Accordingly, reputable dive operators will not permit you to dive on the day on which you plan to fly. You should always leave a gap of at least 12 hours between diving and flying; a 24-hour interval, if practicable, is even better.

INSURANCE
Most holiday insurance policies exclude sports such as scuba diving. It is vital, therefore, that you are properly insured, because a serious incident (although they rarely happen) could involve huge costs.

DIVING FOR THE DISABLED
Aside from the conditions mentioned above, physical disability presents no barrier to learning to dive and all of the dive centres offering training for disabled divers.

Learning to Snorkel

• It takes only a few minutes to learn to snorkel. Once you have mastered the basic techniques, the way is open to hours of pleasure, floating silently over the reefs, watching the many fascinating creatures that live there. Snorkelling is often considered an inferior alternative to scuba diving, but this is a misconception for the following reasons:

• Although scuba allows you to explore deep reefs, there is an enormous amount of colour and life on shallow reefs that can be easily observed from the surface.

• Once you have bought your equipment, snorkelling costs nothing and is easy to organize. You can jump in wherever you want and as often as you like without having to hire tanks or make sure that you have a buddy to dive with. Your time in the water isn't limited by air supply, and you don't have to worry about the dangers of breathing compressed air at depth.

• Some people, for psychological, physiological or other reasons, just never take to scuba diving, while other people find it claustrophobic. If you are one of them, snorkelling is possibly the answer.

GETTING STARTED
• Try out your gear in a swimming pool if you don't feel confident about plunging straight into the sea.

• Make sure stray hairs don't get caught under the fringe of your mask. Unless the edge is flush against your skin, the mask will leak.

• Avoid overtightening the mask strap. Not only will this cause unnecessary wear, it can give you a headache.

• Misting up of the mask can be prevented by rubbing saliva on the inside of the faceplate and then rinsing with sea water. If you are averse to this method, there are anti-misting products on the market which have the same effect.

• If water gets into your mask, simply put your head above the surface and apply pressure to the top rim. The water will run out of the bottom.

• To clear the snorkel of water, put your head above the surface, tilt your head back and exhale vigorously. Always take the next breath slowly, since there may still be a little water left in the snorkel. Another strong blow and your snorkel should be clear.

MOVING THROUGH THE WATER
There are no hard and fast rules about finning, but the 'approved' method, although rather controversial, is that you keep your legs straight, providing maximum efficiency of movement. The 'incorrect' way is to bicycle with your legs – that is, to repetitively draw your knees in before you kick out.

It must be said, however, that although the 'wrong' way may be slightly less efficient, the important thing is that you are comfortable and that you are headed in the direction in which you'd like to go.

Similarly, snorkelling manuals generally tell you not to use your hands and arms for propulsion. Although this is good advice for divers – novices are easily recognized by their flapping arms – for snorkellers it is basically irrelevant. Beneath the surface you may want to supplement straight fin-kicking with breaststroke in order to increase your range, while the fastest way to travel on the surface is to crawl.

FREE DIVING

The term 'free diving' is sometimes used to describe snorkelling in general. In fact, what it means is diving beneath the surface without scuba tanks. Anyone who is fit can, with sufficient practice, reach depths of 7–9m (23–30ft) in the tropics. Local people often go to depths of 21m (69ft) when collecting pearls and the like.

Yellowstripe goatfish usually occur in small shoals.

The most important point to remember when free diving is to equalize the pressure in your ears as you descend. Sometimes they equalize of their own accord. If they don't, simply hold the nosepiece of your mask and blow gently through your nose; this should make your ears 'pop' themselves clear. If your ears hurt it's because they haven't cleared properly – an effect that can be exacerbated by a cold or bad sinuses. Come up and try again: do **not** continue to descend on the assumption that your ears will clear sooner or later.

DRIFT-DIVING

When drift-diving, the dive boat skipper needs to know where to find you. The best way to do this is for the divemaster to tow a line onto which a buoy is attached. The skipper is thus able to follow the divers and can be in immediate contact with them should the weather suddenly change or some other danger arise.

As you go deeper you may feel pressure building up and pushing your mask into your face. To alleviate this, simply exhale gently through your nose.

The best way to go under the surface is to pike dive (surface dive). Bend forward at the waist and lift your legs perpendicular to the surface. The weight of your legs should now cause you to sink until your fins are below the surface. If necessary, augment the dive with a couple of breaststrokes.

Some people, very unwisely, hyperventilate in order to stay underwater for longer periods of time. This involves inhaling and exhaling very deeply several times before you dive. The hazard is that hyperventilation can lead to sudden unconsciousness underwater or even after you have resurfaced and taken another breath. Snorkelling manuals counsel against it, but most snorkellers try it at one time or another, and some do it all the time. Because of the dangers, however, this practice is **definitely not** recommended.

A last point about free diving is often forgotten: as you surface, look upwards – otherwise you might crash into a boat or someone swimming on the surface! Also, look about you, as a boat might be approaching and the driver may not have seen you.

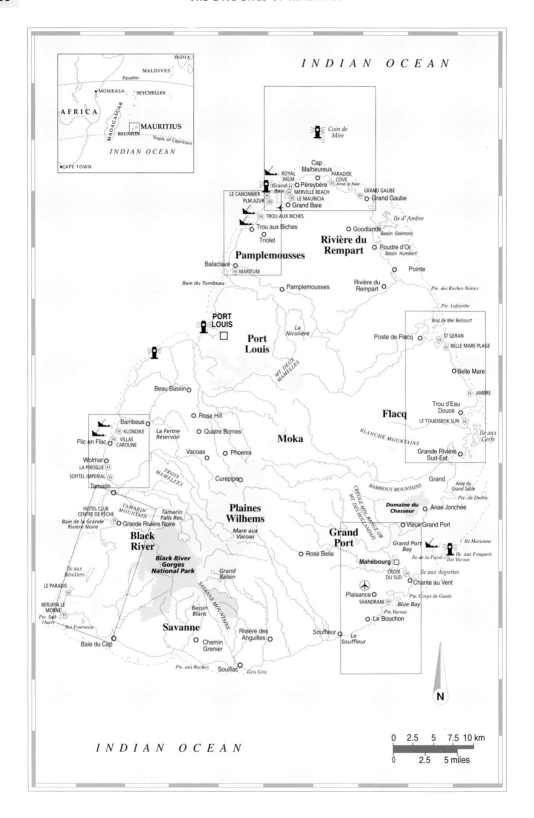

INTRODUCING THE DIVE SITES OF MAURITIUS

The essential purpose of this book is to describe the dive sites and diving conditions that visitors to Mauritius are likely to be exposed to. It deals only with those dive sites that commercial diving centres take their clients to; it does not deal with specialist sites which lie 'off the beaten track' and which therefore require specialist knowledge and equipment. To dive these sites it is necessary to make contact with local Mauritian divers or to make special arrangements with operators who offer specialist diving to suitably qualified divers.

The island has been divided into six subregions, centred on diving areas and the diving centres which serve them. Each subregion is dealt with separately, beginning in the **Southwest** and moving in a clockwise direction. The Southwest includes the Le Morne peninsula and the Black River area, as diving centres are situated in both areas.

The **West** includes the coastal strip made up of the municipal areas of Wolmar and Flic en Flac – some 5km (3 miles) of coastline. All the dive centres are situated at hotels within this area and most of the dive sites occur offshore along this stretch. From the northern border of Flic en Flac through to Pointe aux Piments, north of Port Louis, no organized diving takes place and this stretch of coastline (which only offers specialized diving) therefore falls outside the scope of this book.

The **Northwest** subregion begins at Pointe aux Piments, where the luxury Maritim Hotel and diving centre is situated, and ends at Pointe aux Canonniers. This subregion includes Trou aux Biches – a prime holiday area in Mauritius – where a number of diving centres are located.

From Pointe aux Canonniers, the **North** subregion stretches to Grand Gaube in the east. An almost unbroken ribbon of tourist-related development occurs along this coastline. The greatest concentration of diving centres is found in this subregion and the widest range of dive sites, including diving off the offshore islands north of Mauritius. From Grand Gaube to Poste de Flacq there is no large-scale tourism development and no diving centres exist along this part of the coastline.

For the purposes of this book, the **East** subregion is, therefore, restricted to the Flacq district between Pointe de Flacq, where the St Géran Hotel is situated, to Trou d'Eau Douce where Le Touessrok Hotel is situated. From Trou d'Eau Douce to Pointe Jerome, south of Mahébourg, there are no diving centres and so, again, no organized diving takes place along this relatively deserted coastline.

The **South** subregion has two dive centres: Coral Dive at the Croix du Sud Hotel at Pointe Jerome and the other at the Shandrani Hotel on the shores of Blue Bay. No organized diving takes place along the rest of the island's south coast (from Blue Bay to Le Morne peninsula).

This book concentrates primarily on scuba diving and little reference is made to snorkelling, as this is possible around almost the entire perimeter of the island, either in rock pools or within the aquamarine lagoons that are sandwiched between the offshore coral reefs and the white powder beaches of the island.

THE SOUTHWEST

Diving in the Southwest subregion is concentrated in the area that stretches from just north of Black River to south of the Le Morne peninsula. There are, however, a limited number of sites between Black River and the southern part of Flic en Flac that are also used by diving centres operating in this subregion.

Due to the close proximity of the dive sites the general underwater topography is similar, and, in the main, is made up of a sandy floor dotted with coral patches and rocky outcrops encrusted with flat corals. The main differences lie in the depth of the dive. Most dives take place on the plateau, or continental shelf, lying between the barrier reef and the deep drop-off so typical of volcanic islands. An interesting feature of the reef is that nearly 60 percent of the corals in this subregion display their polyps in daylight while sifting the water for zooplankton. This makes for very interesting macrophotography. Diving in the Southwest, as with diving in much of Mauritius, should be seen for what it is: an opportunity to spend time in an underwater environment that has much beauty, if you make a little effort to look for it. Because most of the corals are, in fact, coral crusts on volcanic rocks, their beauty is subtle, rather than spectacular. To enhance interest the diver should look for interesting colours and formations rather than the dramatic coral structures typical of even warmer tropical waters. Attention should be given to the smaller creatures and tiny fish that live within the corals, for their habits are curious and infinitely fascinating. It is important to approach the Southwest with the motivation of an explorer, rather than that of a spectator.

DIVING CONDITIONS
There is invariably very little current and horizontal visibility averages around 20–25m (66–82ft). In ideal conditions it can reach up to 40m (131ft). The major factor inhibiting visibility is a moderately high level of suspension. Water temperature ranges from 20–22°C (68–72°F) in winter, and 26–30°C (79–86°F) in summer.

Left: *Towering Le Morne Brabant dominates the southwest peninsula.* Above: *The Mauritian anemonefish, or clownfish as it is also known, is found only around the island after which it is named.*

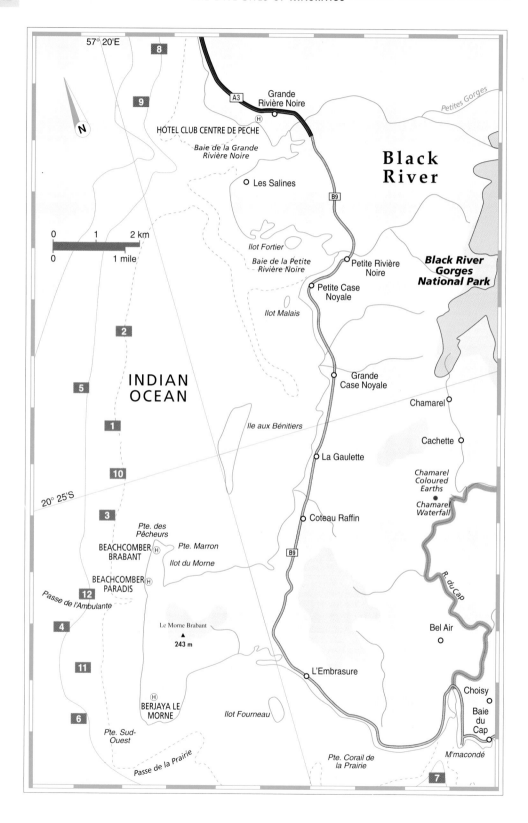

57° 20'E

8

9

HÔTEL CLUB CENTRE DE PECHE

Grande
Rivière Noire

A3

Petites Gorges

**Black
River**

Baie de la Grande
Rivière Noire

Les Salines

B9

0   1   2 km

0   1 mile

Ilot Fortier

Baie de la Petite
Rivière Noire

Petite Rivière
Noire

**Black River
Gorges
National Park**

2

Petite Case
Noyale

Ilot Malais

5

INDIAN
OCEAN

1

Grande
Case Noyale

Chamarel

Ile aux Bénitiers

Cachette

10

La Gaulette

20° 25'S

Chamarel
Coloured
Earths

Chamarel
Waterfall

3

Pte. des
Pêcheurs

Coteau Raffin

BEACHCOMBER
BRABANT

Pte. Marron

Ilot du Morne

R. du Cap

BEACHCOMBER
PARADIS

B9

12

Passe de l'Ambulante

4

Le Morne Brabant
▲
243 m

Bel Air

11

L'Embrasure

BERJAYA LE
MORNE

Choisy

6

Ilot Fourneau

Baie
du
Cap

Pte. Sud-
Ouest

Pte. Corail de
la Prairie

M'macondé

Passe de la Prairie

7

Popular dive sites in the Southwest subregion are:

1 NEEDLE HOLE

★★★

Location: See map.
Access: By boat from any of the dive centres operating in the subregion.
Conditions: Hardly any current. Visibility is between 20 and 25m (66-82ft). Because of the good conditions of the site it is used for orientation and night dives.
Average depth: 12m (39ft)
Maximum depth: 16m (52ft)

An interesting feature of this dive is the congregation of Sergeant-majors (*Abudefduf vaigiensis* and *A. sparoides*) and fusiliers (both *Caesio xanthonotae* and *C. teres*) near the surface of the water; sometimes their dorsal fins actually break the surface. Once divers are submerged they are enveloped in a colourful cloud of these little fish. In order to appreciate the site, divers should proceed slowly and observe the smaller creatures that make up the marine environment. This site is good for wide-angle photography, especially of fish and divers with the coral forming a pretty background. On a clear day when the sun is bright, natural light photography is possible.

2 ANTHONY'S PLACE

★★

Location: See map.
Access: By boat from any of the dive centres operating in the subregion.
Conditions: Diving conditions are generally good; there is invariably very little current and visibility varies between 20 and 25m (66-82ft).
Average depth: 14m (46ft)
Maximum depth: 16m (52ft)

The dive site covers an area of about 1500m² centred on a rock with a coral pinnacle. This rock is surrounded by white coral sands in deep gullies which lead to other rock and coral mounds dotted about the site area.

An interesting feature of this dive is that the area was heavily dynamited about 15 years ago and it is remarkable to see how Nature is steadily healing her dreadful scars. If you look closely at the corals it is possible to see small shrimps and crabs occasionally popping their heads out to stare at the human intruders in their realm.

Sizable clams can be seen on this dive site and if divers approach them stealthily, it is possible to see inside their jaws before they snap shut.

A variety of shells can be found in the gullies, where coral reef and sand meet. Cowries and cone shells are prevalent, but they have to be looked for, and should be left undisturbed after being found.

3 JIM'S PLACE

★★

Location: See map.
Access: By boat from any of the dive centres operating in the subregion.
Conditions: Diving conditions are generally good; there is invariably very little current (depending on the tide) and visibility is good enough for natural light photography.
Average depth: 14m (46ft)
Maximum depth: 16m (52ft)

The site consists of four banks (or fingers) of coral with sand gullies inbetween. A variety of low, hard corals grows on these reefs encouraging a plentiful fish life including goatfish, soldierfish (*Myripristis* spp.), Black-spotted pufferfish (*Arothron nigropunctatus*), the spikey Birdbeak burrfish, otherwise known as the Porcupine fish (*Cyclichthys orbicularis*), and Threadfin butterflyfish (*Chaetodon auriga*). Emperor angelfish (*Pomacanthus imperator*) and Oriental sweetlips (*Plectorhinchus orientalis*) are seen on a fairly regular basis.

Some of the more common fish are Moorish idols (*Zanclus canescens*), swimming in pairs or threesomes, various species of brightly coloured parrotfishes, clownfish tucked into their anemones, shoals of snappers hovering about the reef, and, on most dives, a family of seven Clearfin lionfish (*Pterois radiata*) gather in a small cave in the area.

There are numerous sea urchins with their long spines interspersed amongst the soft corals. During a night dive many of the crayfish (lobsters) that hide in the reef's crevices during the day can also be seen.

FISH ROUTINE

Over half the fish found on most coral reefs are diurnal species, spending most of their daylight hours on the surface of the reef or just above it, sometimes hovering and sometimes patrolling their territory, but always watching out for imminent danger. Others spend their time weaving between outcrops of reef, covering long distances in search of food.

Most of these diurnal fish are colourful and conspicuous and give tropical reefs a sense of vibrancy and a kaleidoscope of absorbing fascination.

The fish that fall readily into this category are most wrasses, damselfish, butterflyfish, surgeonfish, parrotfish, snappers, squirrelfish, triggerfish, hawkfish and goatfish. Now and again a grouper may leave its lair and come flitting past – always an impressive sight!

Nearly one third of all reef fish are cryptic, in other words they prefer to camouflage themselves by blending into their background, and spending most of their time carefully hidden within the structure of the reef. They are seldom noticed by the casual visitor. Typical fish that fit into this category are the blennies, gobies, scorpionfishes (particularly), pipefishes and moray eels.

About one-tenth of reef fish are nocturnal, and only come out at night, usually to search for food. Their days are spent hidden in caves and crevices and they can, therefore, only be seen on night dives.

The balance, of course, is made up of both.

4 CLIFF

★★★

Location: The dive site is situated directly opposite Le Paradis Hotel on the outer edge of the barrier reef. See map.
Access: By boat from any of the diving centres operating in the subregion.
Conditions: The same general conditions apply, but the site can be quite badly affected when there is a strong tidal surge.
Average depth: 22m (72ft)
Maximum depth: 25m (82ft)

This is a small site situated on a sharp drop-off, as the name implies. The scenery is interesting, but not spectacular. Up to four Javanese moray eels (*Gymnothorax javanicus*) are seen on most dives, as well as a fairly comprehensive range of other fish typical of this subregion,

such as snappers, goatfish, Sergeant-majors (*Abudefduf vaigiensis*) and wrasses, of which various species occur in the subregion, the Checkerboard wrasse (*Halichoeres hortulanus*) probably being the most common.

Some of the more prominent species found on this dive are Blueline snappers (*Lutjanus kasmira*) and both Honeycomb and Peacock groupers (*Epinephelus merra* and *Cephalopholis argus*).

5 JAPANESE GARDEN

★★

Location: See map.
Access: By boat from any of the dive centres operating in the subregion.
Conditions: Diving conditions are very similar to the other dive sites: there is very little current (usually tidal) and visibility is good.
Average depth: 14-20m (46-66ft)
Maximum depth: 28m (92ft)

Aptly named for the many and varied colours of the low corals that encrust the rocks in the site area, this dive is usually done down the drop-off, starting at 14m (46ft) and ending at 25m (82ft), although it can quite equally be dived up the drop-off – in other words the other way around. The general consensus, however, is that the best effect can be achieved by slowly wandering downwards. A wide variety of tropical fish can be seen on this dive and perhaps the most prominent amongst these is a variety of butterflyfish, including the Longnosed (*Forcipiger flavissimus*), surgeonfish, juvenile and adult Emperor angelfish (*Pomacanthus imperator*), and various parrotfish. Among the corals there is a great deal of small life to observe, including Pipefish (*Corythoichthys nigripectus*), and coral crabs.

Both Geometric and Ghost moray eels (*Siderea grisea* and *S. prosopeion*) occasionally pop their heads out of their crevice homes to watch you swim past.

6 CASIERS

★★★

Location: See map.
Access: By boat from any of the dive centres operating in the subregion.
Conditions: Diving conditions are very similar to the other dive sites, except that tidal influence is a little more pronounced. Visibility can be adversely affected by suspensions in the water.
Average depth: 26m (85ft)
Maximum depth: 32m (105ft)

Sea fans have a protein base and are usually covered with small polyps.

The name *casiers* means 'fish trap' in Creole, and the site was so-named because its prolific fish population encouraged the setting of many fish traps in the area.

The reef is flat, horseshoe-shaped and covered with low, pretty coral.

It has a fairly representative and attractive range of tropical fish life, such as the Mauritian boxfish (*Ostracion trachys*), the Blue-trim and the Cateau 'Blanc' parrotfish (*Scarus ghobban* and *S. dubius*), and the Black-spotted pufferfish (*Arothron nigropunctatus*).

Picasso and Clown triggerfish (*Rhinecanthus aculeatus* and *Balistoides conspicullum*) are both fairly rare in this subregion, but can sometimes be seen here.

The real reason for visiting this site if you are in the area, however, would be because of the possibility of seeing the big pelagic game fish, such as tuna (*Katsuwonus* sp.), kingfish (*Caranx* sp.) and wahoo (*Acanthocybium solandri*).

Even dolphins have occasionally been spotted in this area, a most unusual but spectacular sight indeed.

In good weather an aerial view of Mauritius reveals an emerald jewel bathed in a turquoise sea. But when the full fury and might of a tropical cyclone descends on the island – which generally only occurs at intervals of about 15 years – the idyllic picture is destroyed: the island turns cruel, attracting ships that are in distress, and ruthlessly casting them onto the spiky coral reefs.

Records show that at least 107 ships have met their fate on the shores of Mauritius, but the number of lives lost is unknown. Of the total number of ships lost, some 48 came to grief in the immediate vicinity of Port Louis and another 30 in the approaches to it, between Flic en Flac and Grand Baie. It is thus the northwest quadrant, the harbour and the approaches to it, that form the island's ship graveyards.

The first fleet known to meet its fate on the island's reef was commanded by Dutch admiral Pieter Both. In 1615 a flotilla of four ships set sail for Holland, heavily laden with merchandise. Shortly after leaving port they were struck by a vicious tropical cyclone. Admiral Both tried to return to the relative safety of Noordt Wester Haven (now Port Louis) but the cyclone drove them backwards, destroying one ship on the reef at Baie du Tombeau, sending another onto the sandbank at Pointe aux Sables and a third, Both's ship *Banda*, onto the reef further south, near Albion. Both and many of his sailors drowned.

World-renowned professional diver Jacques Dumas salvaged the *Banda* in 1979/80, but the remains offer no wreck-diving opportunities for divers today.

MAHEBOURG NAVAL MUSEUM

Perhaps the best known wreck in Mauritius is the *St Géran*: not only has the romance and drama that surrounded it's wrecking provided the inspiration for a classic French love story, but one of the island's most exclusive hotels has been named after it. The two lovers whom Bernardin de Saint-

A typical example of marine growth on a wreck.

Pierre centred his romantic story on, Paul and Virginie, have become legendary. At Poudre d'Or, opposite Ile d'Ambre, an obelisk has been erected by the Historical Society of Mauritius to commemorate the sinking of the *St Géran* in 1744. In 1966 the scattered remains of the ship were discovered by divers and the ship's bell, which is now on display at the Mahébourg Naval Museum, was recovered.

A visit to this museum provides a fascinating insight into the naval and maritime history of the island. It was in Grand Port Bay that a fearsome naval battle took place in 1810 between a squadron of four British frigates (*Sirius*, *Iphigenia*, *Magicienne* and *Nereide*) and a gun brig (HMS *Staunch*), and four ships of the French navy (*Minerve*, *Victor*, *Céylan* and *Bellone*) that were based there. The British gained entry to the bay by capturing the small island, Ile de la Passe, which guarded the entrance to Grand Port Bay. They did this by flying the *tricolor* and deceiving the French garrison stationed there into believing that they were from France. The battle continued for four days. The *Sirius* and the *Magicienne* ran aground and were set alight by their own officers to prevent them from falling into French hands. The *Nereide* was captured by the French and the *Iphigenia* surrendered when reinforcements arrived from Port Louis. British pride was severely dented while the French celebrated their victory by engraving it on the Arc de Triomphe in Paris. It was the only naval battle the French won during the Napoleonic era.

MAURITIUS UNDERWATER GROUP

In 1964 the Mauritius Underwater Group found the remains of the *Sirius*. This ship, which was commissioned in 1797 and built by Dudman's Yard on the Thames, had in its 13 years of life seen a reasonable amount of action. She participated in the Battle of Trafalgar and, it is reported, conducted herself well during that battle. Her remains lie in three sections in shallow water on the seaward side of Petite Pâte, the deep and navigable channel leading into the harbour. The shallowest portion of the wreck lies at 10m (33ft) and is believed to be the bow. Only a few metal objects remain, as those parts of the wooden hull that survived the ship's sinking have long since disintegrated and disappeared. The middle section, which is defined as that part of the ship that lies between the foresail and the mizzenmast, is estimated to be 22m (72ft) long and lies at a depth extending from 16–22m (52–72ft). This section has been identified by the number of cannon balls that were found lying about, and is obviously where the ammunition well was located in the ship. The first divers who located the wreck also found copper sheathing, shackles and various fragments nearby.

The stern section is in deeper water – between 21 and 24m (69-79ft). It lies about 20m (66ft) away from the middle section and marine archaeologists believe that this is accounted for by the violence of the blast that ripped the ship apart when the powder room exploded after the crew had set the ship alight. Again a fair amount of débris endured the damage and the relentless ravaging of the sea for over 150 years – copper sheathing, bronze keel pins, items thought to be rudder gudgeons, nails, bolts, pulleys and even rope were found. Items of war found on the site include cannons, gunflints and trigger guards, while a number of personal effects have been discovered which bring a measure of poignancy to the sifting of evidence from past conflict. Buttons, belt buckles, toilet bottles and copper coins are some of the items the sea has given up to the underwater researchers.

Subsequent to the initial work done on the wreck by the Mauritius Underwater Group, souvenir hunters blasted the wreck with dynamite in the vain hope of finding riches but instead did considerable damage and found little of intrinsic value. The wreck is now protected by the government and is out of bounds to most divers.

MAURITIUS MARINE CONSERVATION SOCIETY

For divers who have limited time and no access to the remote parts of the island where the bones of old ships have come to rest, or who have, perhaps, little interest in marine archaeology but nevertheless a desire to dive on a wreck, the best thing to do is to dive on one of the artificial reefs which have been created by the Mauritius Marine Conservation Society at various points around the island.

Seeing the clearly discernible shape of a ship materialize in the dimness of the underwater world is an experience that must surely cause a ripple to run down the spine of even the most impassive diver! Furthermore it is fascinating to see how the sea steadily clothes man's machines in a mantle of marine organisms and growths while slowly corroding its metal components, turning them into the dust from which they originally came.

Wreck diving adds an interesting and historical dimension to underwater diving, even if the lure of finding hidden treasures no longer has any lustre.

This Giant reef ray has partially buried itself in sand. Rays feed on molluscs and crabs found on the sea bottom.

7 SOUTH BANK or PASSE ST JACQUES

★★★

Location: See map.
Access: By boat from any of the dive centres operating in the subregion.
Conditions: Can become very rough when the southeast winds blow.
Average depth: 20m (66ft)
Maximum depth: 25m (82ft)

This drift dive begins at a fairly shallow 15m (49ft) and slowly descends down a wall to 25m (82ft).

There are few corals because of the steady flow of water through the pass.

The main attraction of the dive site is the thrill of seeing the pelagic game fish (kingfish and tuna), Eagle-rays (*Aetobatus narinari*) and Black-tip sharks (*Carcharhinus melanopterus*).

Reticulate morays (*Myrichthys maculosus*) are also seen in this area from time to time.

8 GORGONIA

★★

Location: See map.
Access: By boat from any of the dive centres operating in the area.
Conditions: Visibility can be poor at low tide, because the dive takes place near the Black River mouth.
Average depth: 16m (52ft)
Maximum depth: 35m (115ft)

The main attraction of this dive site is a single large gorgonian that is more than 3m (10ft) in diameter. In addition to the reef fish typical of the subregion, fusiliers, surgeonfish and pufferfish are common residents, as are Threadfin butterflyfish (*Chaetodon auriga*), Schooling bannerfish (*Heniochus diphreutes*), Emperor angelfish (*Pomacanthus imperator*), the Firegoby (*Nemateleotris magnifica*) and the pretty Oriental sweetlips (*Plectorhinchus orientalis*). As always, be wary of the well-camouflaged stonefish (*Synanceia verrucosa*).

9 CHEMINEE

★★

Location: See map.
Access: By boat from any of the dive centres operating in the subregion.
Conditions: Diving conditions are generally good but occasionally visibility can be impaired by suspension in the water brought down by the river.
Average depth: 20m (66ft)
Maximum depth: 25m (82ft)

This site is located on a small drop-off and follows a plateau at 25m (82ft). The area is covered in low corals and has a fish life that is representative of the subregion, and includes snappers, goatfish, soldierfish (*Myripristis* spp.), surgeonfish (*Acanthurus* spp.), parrotfish, wrasses, butterflyfish and the rarely seen Reticulate morays (*Myrichthys maculosus*). The dive slowly ascends to about 20m (66ft) where a chimney slopes upwards to 17m (56ft). The dive then continues at this level until completion.

10 CASTLE

★★★★ (as a night dive) ★★ (as a day dive)

Location: See map.
Access: By boat from any of the dive centres operating in the subregion.
Conditions: Diving conditions are generally good; there is invariably very little current; visibility is usually good.
Average depth: 15m (49ft)
Maximum depth: 17m (56ft)

This site is often used for night-diving because of the good conditions and the interesting nocturnal marine life, including both Hawksbill and Green turtles which are seen from time to time. As a night dive it is highly recommended, as pretty Spanish dancers *(Hexabranchus sanguineus)* come out of their holes and ripple their way across the reef in search of food; polyps open and the corals take on a magnificent hue. As a day dive, however, it is only worth doing if you are on the spot.

11 LA PASSE

★★★☆☆☆

Location: Diving takes place in a small pass through the barrier reef. See map.
Access: By boat from any of the dive centres operating in the subregion.

Conditions: Since this dive takes place in a pass through which tidal flows are channelled, currents, which can become strong at new moon, can be expected.
Average depth: 12m (39ft)
Maximum depth: 18m (59ft)

The dive site is located in a coral-encrusted area of the reef. The corals are low and colourful, but not spectacular. Perhaps the most outstanding feature of this dive is the wide variety of fish that can be seen.

If you are patient and you watch carefully, it is possible to see virtually all of the following fish: snappers, particularly the Bluebanded (*Lutjanus kasmira*) and Blue-striped (*L. notatus*); goatfish, particularly Yellow-fin (*Mulloides vanicolensis*), Yellowstriped (*M. flavolineatus*), Yellowsaddle (*Parupeneus cyclostomus*) and occasionally Dash-and-dot (*Parupeneus barberinus*); soldierfish (*Myripristis* spp.); Sergeant-majors (*Abudefduf vaigiensis* and *A. sparoides*); surgeonfish (*Acanthurus* spp.); Picasso triggerfish (*Rhinecanthus aculeatus*); Clown triggerfish (*Balistoides conspicullum*); the Checkerboard wrasse (*Halichoeres hortulanus*); Mauritian boxfish (*Ostracion trachys*); Blue-trim parrotfish (*Scarus ghobban*) and the Cateau 'Blanc' parrotfish (*S. dubius*); Black-spotted pufferfish (*Arothron nigropunctatus*); Birdbeak burrfish

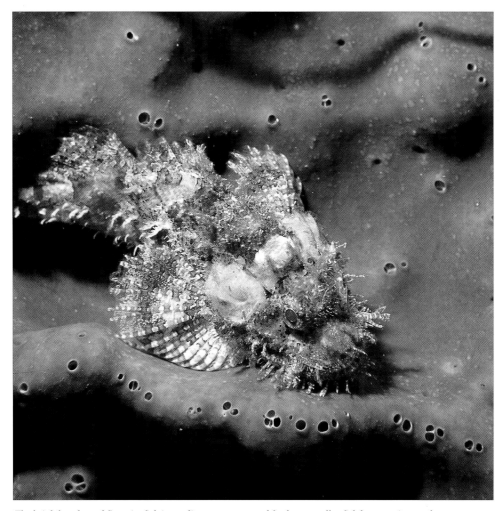

The brightly coloured Scorpionfish is a solitary creature, and feeds on smaller fish by pouncing on them.

(*Chilomycterus orbicularis*); Spotted snake-eels (*Myrichthys maculosus*); Threadfin butterflyfish (*Chaetodon auriga*); Schooling bannerfish (*Heniochus diphreutes*); Emperor angelfish (*Pomacanthus imperator)*; Common stonefish (*Synanceia verrucosa*); Firegoby (*Nemateleotris magnifica*); and Oriental sweetlips (Plectorhinchus orientalis).

Snorkelling is good, but is only possible in the pass when conditions are right.

12 LA MURIANT
★★★

Location: See map.
Access: About 10-20 minutes by boat from any of the dive centres operating in the area.

Conditions: Diving conditions are generally good; there is usually very little current and visibility averages between 20 and 25m (66-82ft).
Average depth: 20m (66ft)
Maximum depth: 24m (79ft)

The dive begins on a shelf at 17m (56ft) and then drops off to 24m (79ft).

The general topography is much the same as the other dive sites in the area, but there are two features that make it particularly interesting: the first is its relatively prolific fish life; as the fish are accustomed to being fed by divers, they gather about in expectation. The second feature is that there are two Giant moray eels (*Gymnothorax javanicus*) which have been resident in the area for years. The one, known as Barbara to some divers, is exceptionally friendly and likes to be fed, while the other is coy and seldom emerges.

COST OF DIVING

The cost of a dive ranges from Rs400-Rs550, depending on the site and on whether or not the diver provides all of his own gear (the supply of a tank and weight belt is included in the basic cost of all dives). The cost of training is about Rs600 for an introduction to diving course, and about Rs6000 for a One-star qualification.

DIVING CENTRES

There are three diving centres which operate in this subregion, two in the Le Morne area and one in Black River:

Diveplan Ltd. trading as Beachcomber Diving Mauritius. Le Paradis Hotel, Le Morne, Case Noyale.
Tel: 683-6775 Fax: 683-6786

The centre provides a service to guests from the Brabant and Paradis hotels, as well as to visitors (providing arrangements are made with the security guard at the entrance to the hotel complex). All qualifications are recognized, but divers must have their diving certificate with them and their log book should be current. (This pertains to all dive centres throughout Mauritius.) If the prospective diver has not dived recently an orientation dive may be necessary.

The centre has sufficient equipment to kit out 10 divers and hires out equipment to divers on request. All gear is either Spirotechnique or Cressi-Sub. Diving tanks are 12-litre aluminium.

The dive boat is a fully equipped 27ft deep-V fibreglass mono-hull powered by twin 90HP motors and can accommodate 10 divers, two divemasters and a skipper in comfort.

The dive centre is affiliated to PADI and offers Open Water and Advanced Open Water training as well as PADI Open Water and Advanced Open Water diver specialities, such as photography, deep diving, wreck-diving and so on. NAUI and CMAS courses are also available. The centre is a registered member of the MSDA.

Easydive Diving Centre. Berjaya Le Morne Beach Resort, Le Morne.
Tel: 683-6800 Fax 683-6070

Easydive has only recently been established. It operates from new premises in which the comfort and needs of the diver have been taken into account. All equipment is Scubapro and the centre can kit out 15 divers completely. Tanks are 12-litre steel. All equipment is supplied and included in the cost of the dive.The centre operates a fully equipped 23.5ft flat-bottomed fibreglass boat, powered by twin 40HP motors.

Easydive is a registered member of the MSDA. It is PADI-affiliated and offers a full range of training including:

• Discover Scuba Diving
• PADI Open Water Diver Course
• PADI Advanced Diver Course
• PADI Rescue
• PADI Divemaster
• PADI Medic First Aid

Odyssee Diving Centre. Centre de Péche, Black River.
Tel: 683-6503 Fax 683-6318

Recently established, this diving club has sufficient equipment to fully kit out five divers. It operates a 21x6ft fibreglass boat which is powered by twin Yamaha 15HP motors.

At present the club is only able to offer an introductory course to diving. In addition to using dive sites in the Le Morne area and in the West subregion (described in the next section) Odyssee has some of its own sites in the Black River area including the following:

• Cheminée (27m, 89ft)
• Gorgonia (33m, 108ft)
• Pointe Koenig (10-18m, 33-59ft)
• Le Pique (3-20m, 10-66ft)

SPORT AND RECREATIONAL ACTIVITIES

Golf
One of the two 18-hole golf courses on the island forms part of the sports facilities available at the Brabant and Paradis hotels in this area.

Watersports
Water-skiing, windsurfing, yachting, riding in a *pedalo*, parasailing and trips in a fibreglass-bottomed boat are offered by most beach hotels.

Social games
Tennis and squash courts, volleyball courts, snooker tables and other social sport facilities are available for guests of the beach hotels.

Deep-sea fishing
Mauritius is world-renowned for marlin fishing. The best months for deep-sea fishing are October to March. Deep-sea angling can be arranged through the hotel reception for guests, and non-residents can make their own arrangements with the following organizations:

• Beachcomber Fishing Club, Le Morne
Tel: 683-6775 Fax: 683-6786

• Black River Sport Fishing Organisation, Auberge de la Rivière Noire
Tel: 683-6547

Hiking
For those who want to stretch their legs and take a hike in the mountains of the southwest, a number of options are available:

• *Le Petrin to Grand Rivière Noire*
This is possibly the most picturesque of all the hikes in Mauritius. It begins at the junction of the Grand Bassin and Curepipe-Chamarel roads at Le Petrin and passes through the Macchabée forest with its pockets of indigenous trees. Then the hike descends to the valley of the Black River Gorges Nature Area and finally ends at the Pavillon de Jade Restaurant on the main coastal road in the southwest.

The walk normally takes between four and five hours.

• *Le Petrin to Tamarin Falls*
This hike also begins at the junction of the Grand Bassin and Curepipe-Chamarel roads at Le Petrin. The route passes mainly through forest until it nears the falls. There are some interesting detours near the falls themselves which are worth exploring.

The hike ends at the very pretty Tamarin falls, from where there is easy access to Curepipe.

Horseriding
Horseriding is offered to guests of the Brabant and Paradis hotels at Le Morne.

THE WEST

This subregion stretches from Black River in the south to north of Flic en Flac. Diving takes place in a fairly concentrated area on the outside of the barrier reef, which is characterized by a series of more-or-less parallel terraces leading to a sharp drop-off. These terraces are made up of boulders and rocks interspersed with small caves, larger caverns, dramatic archways, chimneys and tunnels. In places the terraces widen to form large, flat areas which are covered with various hard corals and a number of small, pink, soft corals. The dead corals are now covered with sand.

Diving in this region can be divided into two categories: shallower diving – down to 35m (115ft) – along the terraces, and deeper diving – down to 60m (197ft) – on the drop-off.

Only well-qualified divers who have recent, proven deep-diving experience are taken on the deep dives – and then only after a gradual build-up to the deeper levels. Due to the specialized nature of these deeper dives and their general nonavailability to unqualified divers (who may be staying in Mauritius for relatively short periods only), they will not be included in the selection of dive sites in this subregion.

DIVING CONDITIONS

Because of the close juxtaposition of the shallower dive sites to one another and the broad similarities of the general topography, diving conditions are largely similar and therefore will not be separately described for each site. Generally all sites have clear water conditions with visibility ranging between 20 and 30m (66–98ft) and in ideal conditions reaching up to 50m (164ft), sometimes even more.

All sites are subject to currents from time to time. Usually they are very gentle and diving is done using an anchor line, but during summer especially, the current can become quite severe and drift diving is the only alternative. Water temperature is the same for each site, ranging from 20–22°C (68–72°F) in winter and 26–28°C (79–82°F) in summer.

Left: The beach at Flic en Flac is one of the best known on the island. Above: Trumpetfish, or flutemouths as they are also known, hang vertically in coral branches, ambushing unsuspecting small fishes on which they feed.

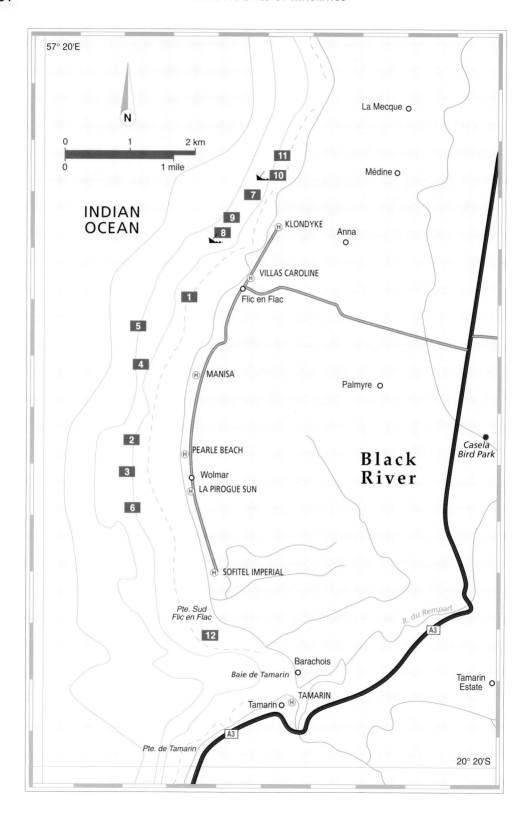

57° 20'E

N

0   1   2 km

0   1 mile

INDIAN
OCEAN

La Mecque ○

Médine ○

11

10

7

9

8

Ⓗ KLONDYKE

Anna
○

Ⓗ VILLAS CAROLINE
○
Flic en Flac

1

5

4

Ⓗ MANISA

Palmyre ○

2

Ⓗ PEARLE BEACH

○ Wolmar
Ⓗ LA PIROGUE SUN

3

6

Ⓗ SOFITEL IMPERIAL

**B l a c k
R i v e r**

Casela
Bird Park ●

Pte. Sud
Flic en Flac

12

R. du Rempart

A3

Barachois
Baie de Tamarin ○

TAMARIN

Tamarin ○ Ⓗ

Tamarin
Estate ○

A3

Pte. de Tamarin

20° 20'S

Popular dive sites in the West sub-region are:

1 AQUARIUM

★★★

Location: See map.
Access: By boat from any one of the dive centres operating in the area. The journey takes approximately 10 minutes, depending on the point of departure.
Conditions: See introduction.
Average depth: 7-12m (23-39ft)
Maximum depth: 19m (62ft)

This is a slow drift dive in shallow water which invariably offers good visibility. The dive starts at 7m (23ft) and descends to 18m (60ft) over large boulders and rocks which are covered in a few places with black coral, various soft corals and small gorgonians.

The principal feature of the dive is the many species of fish that can be seen there, including squirrelfish, soldierfish, various groupers, some of which are infrequent visitors to these waters, such as the Peacock grouper (*Cephalopholus argus*), and there are two large specimens of Moon grouper (*Variola louti*) which are frequently seen in the diving area.

Various species of stonefish and moray eels are seen on virtually every dive and occasionally a Spotted snake-eel (*Myrichthys maculosus*) makes an appearance.

2 CATHEDRAL

★★★★

Location: See map.
Access: By boat from any one of the dive centres operating in the subregion. The journey takes approximately 10 minutes, depending on the point of departure.
Conditions: See introduction.
Average depth: 22m (72ft)
Maximum depth: 27m (89ft)

This dive takes place on the drop-off. It begins at 18m (59ft) at the top of a rock formation that drops steeply along two connecting cliffs to a depth of 27m (89ft). Use a torchlight while descending to enable you to peer deeply into the many interesting cracks and crevices in the rock face that play host to an interesting array of smaller marine creatures.

The dive proceeds into a high chamber and the water becomes warmer – a welcome relief in the winter months. Within the chamber there are large quantities of crayfish and shrimps. The dive culminates in a huge cave

that opens at the rear. This submarine cavern, whose doorkeeper is a huge but shy Giant moray eel (*Gymnothorax javanicus*), has gentle, diffused light filtering through from a crack in its ceiling, creating a feeling of being in the high-vaulted interior of a Gothic cathedral. There is invariably movement in open waters when you are diving, but within the cavern the water is calm and peaceful, and the diver should use this opportunity to pause and look about. It is possible to see soldierfish (*Myripristis* spp.), squirrelfish (*Sargocentron* spp.) and lionfish (*Pterois antennata and P. radiata*), which, with their long antennae, provide a spectacular sight. Occasionally a shoal of kingfish, and the Giant trevally (*Caranx ignobilis*), may enter the cave and mill about, as if seeking refuge. Although the rocks are covered in a variety of marine growths, surprisingly few corals have locked on to them. Of those that have done so, fire corals are the most dominant.

Besides the chamber and its interleading 'cathedral', the site has many nooks and crannies that add to the general attraction of the dive.

3 COULINE BAMBOU

★★ to ★★★★ (depending on diving conditions)

Location: See map.
Access: By boat from any one of the dive centres operating in the subregion. The journey takes about 10 minutes, depending on the point of departure.
Conditions: See introduction.
Average depth: 25m (82ft)
Maximum depth: 34m (112ft)

This is an interesting dive that takes you through a kaleidoscope of changing scenery; it begins at 18m (59ft) with a slow descent down the rocky walls of the drop-off, then up through a chimney which leads out and under a bridge of stone covered in a variety of marine growths. From there divers slowly make their way through a large crack in a rock, down the drop-off to another bridge, where the dive eventually culminates at 34m (112ft). The changing topography makes this an attractive and varied dive. When the current gathers and becomes strong, the character of this dive changes; a lee, where water remains calm, is created within a basin formed by the rocks. Fish collect in the basin and predators follow their trail. And so the diver, if very lucky, is treated to a spectacle of White-tip reef sharks (*Triaenodon obesus*) and tuna (*Thunnus* sp.) going about their deadly business of hunting their prey. When conditions are good, kingfish, Giant reef rays (*Taeniura melanospilos*) and Grey reef sharks (*Carcharhinus amblyrhynchos*) can be seen – but their presence can never be guaranteed. There is, however, a constant variety of interesting reef life to fascinate the diver along the way.

4 MANIOC

★★★

Location: See map.
Access: By boat from any one of the dive centres operating in the subregion. The journey takes approximately 10 minutes, depending on the point of departure.
Conditions: See introduction.
Average depth: 35m (115ft)
Maximum depth: 45m (148ft)

This is a deep dive that starts at 32m (105ft) and descends, for those who have the skill and are properly equipped, to 45m (148ft). The dive site comprises a huge rock on which there are large branched corals (*Tubastrea micrantha*), while pink corals (*Stylaster* sp.) and large pink gorgonians decorate its sides. A variety of game fish can be seen on the dive, including kingfish (both *Caranx ignobilis* and *C. sexfasciatus*), barracuda and tuna. Large Emperor angelfish (*Pomacanthus maculosus*) are frequently seen. Occasionally White-tip sharks (*Triaenodon obesus*) make an appearance. At 45m (148ft) there is a huge cave full of resident crayfish (lobsters).

5 REMPART L'HERBE
also known as SHARK PLACE

★★★★

Location: See map.
Access: By boat from any one of the dive centres operating in the area. The journey takes approximately 10 minutes, depending on the point of departure.
Conditions: See introduction.
Average depth: 45m (148ft)
Maximum depth: 54m (177ft)

The dive is located on a steep, sloping rock pinnacle that can be circumnavigated. The rock is covered in pink and black coral and yellow gorgonians and the whole area abounds in tropical reef fish.

The principal feature of the dive is the number of Grey reef sharks (*Carcharhinus amblyrhynchos*) that are frequent visitors to the site area. These sharks, if approached with a minimum of movement and water disturbance, will allow divers to swim reasonably close to them – certainly close enough to obtain a decent photograph (don't forget your camera). Occasionally Hammerhead sharks (both *Sphyrna mokarran* and *S. zygaena*) can be seen silhouetted against the surface of the sea in the distance. Tuna (*Gymnosarda unicolor*), barracuda (*Sphyraena* spp.) and kingfish (principally *Caranx sexfasciatus*) often swim in large shoals through the dive area. Another visitor to the site is the Almaco kingfish (*Seriola*

CORALS AND THEIR SEX LIFE

There are male coral polyps and there are female coral polyps, and sometimes there are those which are both, or hermaphrodite. Once a year there is a big night when mating occurs, but the build-up takes six months or even longer. During this period the eggs are formed and steadily ripen. At first the eggs are white, but as they mature they change colour to vivid shades of pink, red or orange. At the same time testes are formed in the male polyps and sperm is developed.

But the climatic conditions must also be right: the event usually occurs as spring turns to summer, the water temperature is warm, tidal variation is minimal, the sea is calm and the moon is full. As the event works towards a climax the eggs and sperm of the respective corals are 'bundled' together and half an hour or so before spawning they are 'set'; in other words they are held ready at the mouth of the polyps and can be seen, under the right conditions, through a thin tissue across the mouth. And then, as if a starter's gun has gone off, the polyps across the reefs release their eggs and sperm at the same time, and these gently float up to the surface. Divers who have been privileged to witness this spectacle of Nature have likened this happening to a sensation similar to watching an upside-down snow storm.

Once the bundles reach the surface they break open and the sperm swims off to find an egg of the same coral type. This is a time of frenzied activity as each sperm cell searches out a mate, and when this happens, fertilization takes place. Once it has, the egg cells begin to divide and within a day or so they become swimming coral larvae, known as planulae. These planulae drift about in the sea for a few days, seeking out a suitable place in a coral of the right type, and when this is found they settle down and a new coral colony begins to grow.

rivoliana) – an easy fish to identify because of the black stripe beginning at its snout, crossing its eye and terminating in front of the dorsal fin; it is important to keep a watchful eye on your surrounds to ensure that you don't miss the unforgettable experience of seeing these stream-lined denizens of the deep come swiftly and silently by.

Giant reef rays (*Taeniuira melanospilos*) and Spotted eagle-rays (*Aetobatus narinari*) are also seen fairly frequently. If you look carefully you will always have the privilege of seeing at least one or two groups of the very rare black-and-yellow-striped Indian butterflyfish (*Chaetodon mitratus*) and the Harlequin grouper (*Cephalopholis polleni*).

The Queen coris is a colourful member of its family, found mainly along the reefs of Mauritius's offshore islands.

6 L'EVEILLE

★★

Location: See map.
Access: By boat from any one of the dive centres operating in the area. The journey takes about 10 minutes, depending on the point of departure.
Conditions: See introduction.
Average depth: 27m (89ft)
Maximum depth: 30m (98ft)

The dive can be tackled in two ways, depending on the direction of the prevailing current: if the current is northerly, then divers descend initially to the lowest point of the dive and gradually ascend over a series of small drop-offs or terraces on which patches of anemones are surrounded by attendant Mauritian anemonefish (*Amphiprion chrysogaster*). The distinguishing feature of the Mauritius anemonefish is that it has little yellow coloration along its belly and its anal fin is black.

Small shoals of Lunar fusiliers (*Caesio lunaris*) as well as Blue-and-gold fusiliers (*Caesio teres*) decorate the site with their vivid, contrasting colours. Shoals of unicornfish (*Naso hexacanthus*) are not uncommon, and Bloch's

bigeye (*Priacanthus blochii*) can be seen hiding in corners within the rocks. Because of the vulnerability of the drift dive to the north, dive centre operators tend to reserve its use for experienced divers and photographers.

The drift dive to the south does not have the same fish life, but it does have its own appeal. The dive begins on a flat, coral-covered reef. A variety of honeycomb, brain, small plate and various other corals can be seen, while purple soft corals occasionally break the monotony of colour. But as one progresses further south, the flat reef suddenly gives way to contorted rock formations which combine to form a series of steps leading to the drop-off. On these rocks there are giant oyster-clams which snap shut the instant they feel threatened. At the end of the dive there is a large archway through which divers pass before rising sharply up a small rock face that leads to the surface.

Gathered inside the archway are clouds of Blue-banded snappers (*Lutjanus kasmira*), Yellowfin goatfish (*Mulloides vanicolensis*), Yellowspot emperors (*Gnatho-dentex aureolineatus*) and White-edged soldierfish (*Myripristis murdjan*). Hiding beneath them in the large corrugations created by the current passing over the sea's floor are neatly 'parked' rows of Yellowstriped goatfish (*Mulloides flavolineatus*) – unfazed by their human guests, they seem, in fact, disdainful of their presence.

The Crown-of-Thorns starfish (*Acanthaster planci*) is about 30cm (12in) in diameter and has up to 23 arms which are covered on the dorsal surface with short, fat spines measuring some 3–5cm (1.2–2in) in length. These venomous spines can induce a nasty skin rash, or nausea and severe pain. The species varies in colour from orange to a greenish-blue and purple.

A female Crown-of-Thorns starfish can produce 12–24 million eggs annually. Rapidly increasing populations of this coral predator first gained notoriety in the late 1960s, when it was observed to be causing massive coral-reef destruction. Areas most affected were the Indo-Pacific region, particularly on Australia's Great Barrier Reef, and the reefs of southern Japan. Later observations indicated that the problem was spreading to the islands of Micronesia (especially Guam) and, to a lesser extent, to the Red Sea. These observations caused deep concern amongst scientists and environmentalists: some blamed the depletion of the creature's predators, such as the Triton shell, the pufferfish, the triggerfish and the Humphead wrasse; others pointed out that many of the worst-hit areas had been affected by blast-fishing, harbour construction, dredging and pollution – with a consequent decline in the starfish's natural enemies, such as certain coral species that eat *A. planci* at the egg and larval stage.

However, analysis of core samples drilled through the Great Barrier Reef suggests that such population explosions have occurred regularly throughout history, and it may simply be that with the ever-increasing popularity of scuba diving, many more divers and marine scientists are exposed to a problem that has, in fact, always existed.

The stark white skeletons of *Acropora* corals that have been killed by aggregations of *A. planci* are an ugly and pathetic sight, and many attempts have been made to eradicate the cause of this destruction, but none has ever been fully effective: damaged Crown-of-Thorns soon regenerate, and the

The Crown-of-Thorns starfish – beautiful to behold, but devastating to coral reefs, particularly Staghorn (opposite).

injection of deadly chemicals such as formaldehyde, copper sulphate or sodium hypochlorite is an expensive, slow and inefficient procedure. The only successful extermination tactic has been to bring them ashore and bury them – or, better still, to burn them.

This exceptionally beautiful starfish becomes destructive and ugly *en masse*. The Crown-of-Thorns devours only the live coral tissues, leaving an ugly and forlorn coral skeleton in its wake. It feeds on the polyps, preferably those of *Acropora* table corals, by everting its stomach over the coral so that the digestive enzymes come into direct contact with the coral tissue; thus digestion begins before the food is taken into the mouth. (These enzymes may be the cause of the severe skin reaction suffered by divers who pick up these creatures with their bare hands.)

The Crown-of-Thorns starfish regularly returns to the same coral table until the table is dead. Newcomers are seemingly lured to the coral table by an attractant chemical which is given off during feeding. Usually nocturnal feeders, these starfish prefer to hide deep in crevices during the day, but when aggregations occur, less effort is made to hide – they simply crawl into the shade of the coral table's underside. Other starfish can be seen before dusk moving through shady areas towards their prey.

Various surveys have been carried out in Mauritius in order to determine the extent of the rapid population increase of the Crown-of-Thorns starfish.

Towards the end of 1990 members of the Marine Conservation Division of the Ministry of Agriculture, Fisheries and Natural Resources observed an invasion of this starfish at Balaclava in the north of the island. At the time, the Marine Conservation Division was working with Canadian consultants to establish a permanent reef-monitoring station there. The survey, which was conducted from December through to February of the following year, revealed that the Crown-of-Thorns starfish does indeed pose a potential threat to the coral reefs of Mauritius.

Although invasion is uncommon and localized, it remains one of the topmost stress factors affecting Mauritian coral reefs, and, the Ministry's report added, warrants attention and careful monitoring.

Devil firefish have spines and tentacles projecting from the head, earning the fish its alternative name, Lionfish.

7 REMPART SERPENT

★★★★★

Location: North of La Pirogue Hotel, beyond the barrier reef (see map).

Access: Access to the site, which is restricted, is provided only by one of the following three diving centres: La Pirogue; Klondike; or Villas Caroline.

Conditions: See introduction.

Average depth: 25m (82ft)

Maximum depth: 25m (82ft)

This site comprises a seaweed-covered rocky patch which is approximately 100m (328ft) long and resembles a large snake moving across the sand.

The reef has a comprehensive range of typical tropical fish, a good proportion of which are juveniles. For some extraordinary reason this patch of reef also has the widest range of stonefish, scorpionfish, lionfish and moray eels seen in Mauritius and possibly even the world. The range includes Humpbacked or Devil scorpionfish (*Scorpaenopsis gibbosa*), Bearded (*S. barbata*) and the extremely rare Weedy scorpionfish (*Rhinopias frondosa*), Decoy scorpionfish (*Iracundus signifer*) and the Mauritius scorpionfish (*Sebastapistes mauritiana*), Indian lionfish or Devil firefish (*Pterois miles*), Clearfin lionfish (*P. radiata*), Indian walkman or Dragonfly firefish (*Inimicus filamentosus*), Ocellated dwarf lionfish (*Dendrochirus biocellatus*), Leaf fish (*Taeniatus triacanthus*), Indian waspfish (*Ablabys binotatus*), Common stonefish (*Synanceia verrucosa*), Leopard (*Gymnothorax undulatus*), Yellowmouth (*G. nudivomer*) and Yellowedged (*G. flavimarginatus*) moray eels, as well as Whitemouth (*G. meleagris*), and Snowflake (*Echidna nebulosa*) moray eels.

It is this wide variety of specialized fish life that makes this a five-star site for those who are interested in a marine extravaganza. However, due to the site's fragility and the need to reduce disturbance to an absolute minimum, combined with the inherent dangers the site can present to the uninitiated, access is restricted to experienced divers only. Approximately 15-20m (49-66ft) south of the reef is a fantastic table of coral (*Acropora* sp.) surrounded by Bannerfish (*Heniochus acuminatus*), and within its cracks and crevices there are invariably a number of juvenile lionfish.

8 *KEI SEI 113*

★★★

Location: See map.
Access: By boat from any one of the dive centres operating in the area. The journey takes approximately 10 minutes, depending on point of departure.
Conditions: See introduction.
Average depth: 35m (115ft)
Maximum depth: 40m (131ft)

The *Kei Sei 113* was sunk to form an artificial reef. Partially converted from a barge into a restaurant, it has a strange-looking superstructure built on its deck.

Sunk in 1988, it is partially covered with corals, especially black corals on the starboard side of the ship. There is an interesting fish life around the wreck which includes Circular batfish (*Platax orbicularis*), Giant moray eels (*Gymnothorax javanicus*) which have set up home in the barge, Red snappers (*Lutjanus bohar*), various soldierfish and trumpetfish species, Hawkfish (*Oxycirrhites typus*), and Spotted sweetlips (*Plectorhinchus picus*) which congregate under the boat.

The *Kei Sei 113* can be dived as a single dive or it can be combined with the Park, which is described below.

9 PARK

★★★

Location: See map.
Access: By boat from any one of the dive centres operating in the area. The journey takes approximately 10 minutes, depending on point of departure.
Conditions: Visibility is normally very good, sometimes up to 50m (164ft). The site is subject to a slight current, which invariably runs from north to south and only very occasionally from south to north.
Average depth: 38m (125ft)
Maximum depth: 41m (135ft)

Park comprises a relatively small patch of magnificent coral, which is made up largely of *Montipora* sp., *Lobophyllia* sp. and black coral. This small, natural marine park is situated just to the southwest of the *Kei Sei 113*. The corals are inhabited by a wide variety of fish including shoals of Blue-striped snappers (*Lutjanus notatus*), Bigeyes and other species of soldierfish.

This site can be dived on its own or as part of a dive to the *Kei Sei 113*, depending on the strength of the prevailing current.

It is interesting to note that the marine life on Park has become prolific since the sinking of both the *Kei Sei 113* and the *St Gabriel* some 150m (492ft) to the

southwest. This suggests that the creation of these artificial reefs not only stimulates growth of marine life on the wreck, but also in adjacent areas through some form of symbiotic relationship.

WRECK-DIVING ETHICS

Remember that while diving it is unethical as well as illegal to pick up, move, remove, alter or destroy anything you may find on a wreck.

Be careful not to touch the metal of a wreck because of the dangerous stinging organisms that congregate there.

---

10 *TUG II*

★★★

Location: See map.
Access: By boat from any one of the dive centres operating in the subregion. Journey time is approximately 15 minutes, depending on point of departure.
Conditions: See introduction.
Average depth: 15m (49ft)
Maximum depth: 20m (66ft)

The *Tug II*, which was also sunk to form an artificial reef, has been at the bottom of the sea for over 14 years and a reasonable growth of seaweed and coral has developed on her rusting frame.

The little ship, which could almost be described as 'cute', makes an attractive picture lying on a large expanse of flat sands and, at first glance, has no visible signs of life. But on close examination you will see Freckled garden eels (*Gorgasia maculata*) which make their wispy, cobra-like appearances out of the sand surrounding the wreck.

The ship itself is alive with a constant cloud of busy fish about it. Besides the typical range of small tropical fish, such as a variety of damselfish, butterflyfish and wrasses, there are sizable shoals of Blue-striped snappers, an occasional Bluefin grouper (*Epinephelus flavocaeruleus*), Dash-and-dot goatfish (*Parupeneus barberinus*) and Common bigeyes (*Priacanthus hamrur*). Indian lionfish, which are also known as Devil firefish (*Pterois volitans*), can be seen in the wreck itself while stonefish are found all around the wreck.

Lying next to the hulk is the ship's funnel, which separated from the vessel during a cyclone. Make sure that you look carefully inside it because, if you are lucky, you will see exquisite juvenile Pineconefish (*Monocentris japonicus*) hiding there.

REMPART CANON

★★

Location: See map.
Access: By boat from any of the dive centres operating in the area.
Conditions: See introduction.
Average depth: 16m (52ft)
Maximum depth: 21m (69ft)

There are two interesting aspects to this dive. The first is a cannon lying on a shelf at 12m (39ft) which is from the *Banda*, Admiral Pieter Both's ship, wrecked during a storm in 1615 (*see* page 48 for more details). The actual wrecking did not take place on the site of the cannon. The cannon was, instead, moved fairly recently to the dive site from its original location some distance away where the ship came to rest nearly 400 years ago.

This was done to make the cannon more accessible as the location of the actual wreck is not suitable for recreational diving. The second point of interest in this dive is a large overhang situated further down, under which a large variety of mainly juvenile fish congregate. These include Semicircle angelfish (*Pomacanthus semicirculatus*), Powderblue surgeonfish (*Acanthurus leucosternon*), Black triggerfish (*Melichthys niger*), Dotty triggerfish (*Balistoides viridescens*), Clown triggerfish (*Balistoides conspicillum*) and Yellowspotted burrfish (*Cyclichthys spilostylus*).

DOLPHIN POINT

★★★

Location: The site is situated at the end of the barrier reef, where it gives way to the sweep of Tamarin Bay.
Access: By boat from the Sofitel Diving Centre.
Conditions: This site is influenced by water flows from the Tamarin River. Visibility is normally around 20-25m (65-80ft), but this drops when the river is in flood.
Average depth: 25m (82ft)
Maximum depth: 40m (131ft)

The dive begins on a low coral shelf at 17-18m (56-59ft) and then proceeds down the drop-off to 40m (131ft) where it meets the sandy floor of the channel created by the Tamarin River. Here dolphin can usually be seen in the early morning, often treating the divers to a display of swimming skill, power and grace that is as exhilarating as it is spellbinding. Sometimes, however, the only knowledge divers may have of their presence is their strange, high-pitched call in the distance. On the wall of the drop-off are two friendly groupers, who seldom fail to make an appearance when divers pay a visit to their domain. Scorpionfish (*Scorpaenopsis venosa* and *S. gibbosa*) decorate the drop-off and can be seen on virtually every dive. Yellowfin tuna (*Thunnus albacares*), kingfish, barracuda and a variety of other game fish are usually seen on most dives. As this is a deep dive only experienced divers are taken there.

The Crescent-tail bigeye is found in lagoon pinnacles and on outer reef slopes, feeding on zooplankton.

COST OF DIVING

The cost per dive ranges from Rs400 to Rs800, depending on equipment hire, negotiated packages and whether it is a day or night dive.

DIVING CENTRES

The West is served by the following Mauritius Scuba Diving Association (MSDA) affiliated diving centres:

• **La Pirogue Diving Centre**,
La Pirogue Hotel, Flic en Flac.
Tel: 453-8450 Fax: 453-8449

This is a PADI diving centre which is also CMAS-affiliated. It operates from a convenient and well-appointed site. The centre has a full range of Scubapro and US Divers equipment and is geared to completely kit out 10 divers. Both steel and aluminium tanks are supplied in 10-, 12- and 15-litre capacities. The centre operates a 26ft flat-bottomed fibreglass Boston Whaler, powered by twin 85HP Yamaha motors, and is fully equipped with all necessary first-aid equipment, including oxygen.

La Pirogue Diving School offers comprehensive diver training, including:

• Resort Diving Course (an introductory course to diving)
• PADI Open Water Diver course
• PADI Advanced Diver Course
• PADI Peak Bouyancy Specialty

• **Klondike Diving Centre**,
Klondike Hotel, Flic en Flac.
Tel: 453-8335 Fax: 453-8337

Only recently established, the centre has Scubapro and Beuchat equipment and is able to fully equip five divers. The boat operated by the centre is a 21x7ft fibreglass flat-bottomed boat, powered by twin 25HP motors. Training is provided, ranging from an introductory resort diving course through to One-Star certification. Night dives can be arranged by request. The centre is CMAS-affiliated.

• **Villas Caroline Diving Centre** (also known as Exploration Sous-Marine), Villas Caroline Beach Hotel.
Tel: 453-8539 Fax: 453-8144

The diving centre is situated at the Villas Caroline holiday complex, which has self-contained holiday units (in addition to the hotel accommodation), where people tend to stay longer than they normally do in hotels.

This is very convenient as much of the diving done by the centre is specialist and deep diving – average is 30m (98ft) and maximum 60m (197ft) – and therefore time is needed to become fully 'acclimatized' and to build up the experience appropriate to this form of diving. The centre has two compressors, 30 12-litre steel tanks and is able to fully equip 12 divers, although the maximum number of divers taken is 10 per dive. A 24ft twin-engined boat is used, which is fully equipped with all the necessary first-aid requirements, including oxygen.

The centre is affiliated to CMAS. It does not offer beginner training. A recent medical certificate and proof of diving qualifications are required. The centre is owned and managed by Pierre Szalay, who is President of MSDA and a member of the CMAS International Instructors Association.

• **Sofitel Diving Centre**,
Sofitel Imperial Hotel, Flic en Flac.
Tel: 453-8700 Fax: 453-8320

This dive centre operates from well-appointed premises at the luxury Sofitel Imperial Hotel and caters primarily, but not exclusively, for guests of the hotel. The centre uses Spirotechnique equipment, has 16 12-litre tanks and can fully kit out 12 divers.

However the centre prefers to restrict the number of divers to six per dive. It operates a 24ft Tremlett flat-bottomed boat, which is powered by two motors, one of 15HP and the other 25HP. The centre is CMAS-affiliated and offers training from a basic introductory course to Two-Star certification. Sofitel offers both a video and stills photographic service to clients. It has a Super 8 underwater video camera for hire, or alternatively the divemaster will make a video of clients on their dive. Transfer to VHS is done at the centre. On the other hand, should clients prefer a photograph of themselves underwater, or wish to do their own underwater photography, there is a Nikonos IVA for hire.

SPORT AND RECREATIONAL ACTIVITIES

Watersports
Water-skiing, windsurfing, yachting, riding in a *pedalo*, parasailing and trips in a fibreglass-bottomed boat are offered by most hotels. Facilities are usually available to nonresidents as well, and enquiries should be made at reception or at the hotel's boathouse.

All resort hotels have swimming pools around which residents can laze if they prefer to avoid the beach sand.

Social games
Most beach hotels have tennis and volleyball courts, and indoor snooker rooms and board games for those who would like to escape the sunshine.

Deep-sea fishing
Mauritius is world-renowned for marlin fishing. The best months for deep-sea fishing are October to March. Trips can be arranged through reception for hotel guests, and nonresidents can make their own arrangements with the following organizations:

• Centre de Pêche de l'Ile Maurice, Rivière Noire.
Tel: 683-6552 Fax: 683-6318

• La Pirogue Big Game Fishing, Flic en Flac.
Tel: 453-8441 Fax: 453-8449

• Sofitel Imperial Big Game Fishing, Wolmar.
Tel: 453-8700 Fax: 453-8320

EATING OUT

All hotel tariffs are structured on a dinner, bed and breakfast basis; guests therefore seldom eat out. This is not to say that Mauritius isn't filled with a number of exciting restaurants at which tourists are welcome: probably the most popular restaurant in Flic en Flac is **Sea Breeze** which offers an exciting Chinese fondue; its seafood is also highly recommended. Villas Caroline has a good restaurant, as does the Klondike Hotel. Other restaurants in the area are **Mer de Clurie**, **Le Flamboyant** and the **Golden Horse**.

Port Louis, cosmopolitan capital of this tiny Indian Ocean island, shows a modern face in its high-rise buildings, and a rural face in its colourful street markets.

A visit to the island's capital is a must. The city is an amalgam of the old and new, of East and West, of the First World and the Third World. New tall buildings punctuate the city's skyline and it is clearly evident that Port Louis is trying to break with some of its shackles of the past – but they still retain their grip in many places.

It is a bustling, noisy city and yet a place where people still have time to greet one another and to smile.

One road up from the harbour is the central market, which has the attraction of a robust Third World market and the exotic charm of an oriental bazaar. The entrance gates date back to 1844 and are a wonderful example of pure Victoriana. It is possible to buy almost anything at the market – from food to clothing, manufactured goods to handcrafts and trinkets. Here a sale is not the mundane exchange of goods for cash; it is more a battle of wits and the interplay of tactics between buyer and seller.

Chinatown, which is adjacent to the city's market, is an interesting place to meander through with its quaint and often delapidated shops.

Besides the fascination of wandering around and watching people at work, a visit to the Mauritius Institute in La Chaussée, which is next to the Treasury building, is worthwhile. At the Natural History Museum on the ground floor is a replica of the dodo – a large, flightless bird of the pigeon family that became extinct within the first 100 years of man's arrival on the island. On the second floor is the National Library. Both the library and the museum are closed on Thursdays.

Next to the Mauritius Insititute is the Jardin des Compagnies, which was the French East India Company's vegetable garden in the 1800s. Today it has long avenues of tall banyan tress with large aerial roots. Bottle palms and other trees of botanical interest are also to be found there,

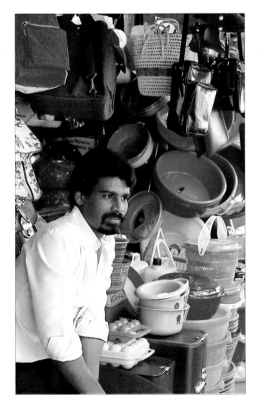

and together they provide very welcome shade to pedestrians in the hot Mauritian sun. A number of statues of people who played a prominent role in Mauritian history line the walkways through the Jardin, and by understanding who they were and what they represented provides an interesting insight into the island's past.

At Plaine Verte in Sir Seewoosagur Ramgoolam Street is a small wooden house hidden by a high brick wall. This is where Dr Maurice Cure was born; the house was also occupied by the late Sir Seewoosagur Ramgoolam between 1936 and 1965. Two years after the death of this greatly admired and revered leader, the house was declared a national monument and converted into a museum, which has been named the Sir Seewoosagur Ramgoolam Memorial Centre for Culture. Many of the leader's personal belongings, including his surgical instruments and other items from his medical career, as well as memorabilia from his political career, are displayed here.

THE NORTHWEST

The Northwest subregion stretches from Pointe aux Piments in the south to Pointe aux Canonniers in the north. It is a popular holiday area with long, uninterrupted beaches that are lined with filaos trees. Lining the beach, from Trou aux Biches to Pointe aux Canonniers, is an almost continuous ribbon of hotel and holiday accommodation.

At Mont Choisy, where relatively thick plantations of *filaos* trees skirt a popular public beach, there is a grassy football pitch where two French pilots, Hily and Scutel, made aviation history in 1933 when they took off from here to fly to Réunion some 160km (99 miles) away to the south. At Mont Choisy Farm, which is nearby, there is a delightful colonial residence; for those who are doing their own catering, it is worth knowing that farm-fresh poultry, meat and giant prawns can be purchased there.

The Dutch used to call Pointe aux Canonniers *De Vuyle Hoek* (the filthy corner), because so many of their ships came to grief on the reefs that lurk beneath the sea's surface. The French established a naval battery on the headland at Pointe aux Canonniers, and some of their cannons, dating back to 1750, are still there, silently pointing out to sea.

A lighthouse was also established at the Point, and is a national monument today.

DIVING CONDITIONS

Because of its situation the area is generally well protected from the prevailing winds from the southeast and can, as a result, offer virtually year-round diving. The area is characterized by a sandy sea bottom, and most diving is done either on rocky outcrops or along the barrier reef, and on the drop-off – which invariably involves deep diving. In addition to using dive sites within this subregion, some of the diving centres operating here also use many of the dive sites in the Grand Baie area in the North subregion.

Water temperatures are generally the same throughout the subregion and range from 19–22°C (66–72°F) in winter and from 26–30°C (79–86°F) in summer.

Left: *Trou aux Biches is a picture of sapphire-blue seas, flame trees and palm-fringed beaches.* Above: *With its pincer appendages, a cleaner shrimp removes unwanted growths from fish, obtaining food for itself in the process.*

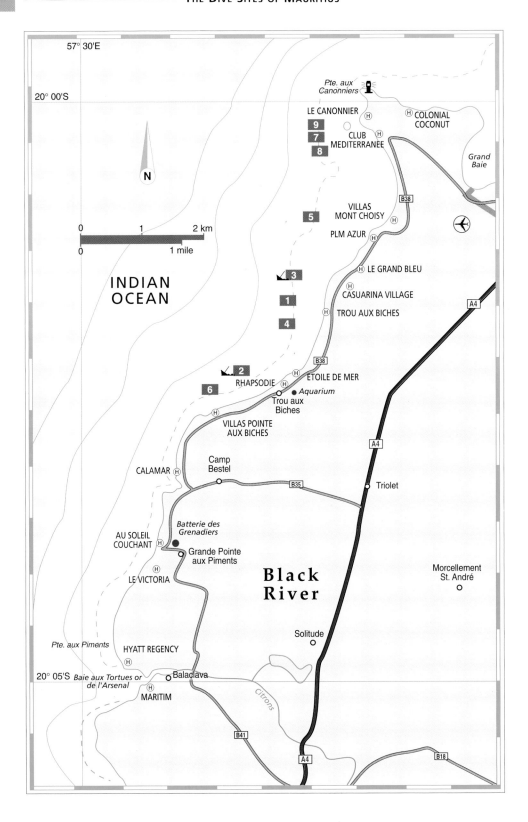

57° 30'E

20° 00'S

Pte. aux Canonniers

LE CANONNIER

9
7
8

COLONIAL COCONUT

CLUB MEDITERRANEE

Grand Baie

N

B38

VILLAS MONT CHOISY

5

PLM AZUR

0   1   2 km
0   1 mile

INDIAN OCEAN

LE GRAND BLEU

3

CASUARINA VILLAGE

1

TROU AUX BICHES

A4

4

B38

2

ETOILE DE MER

6

RHAPSODIE

Aquarium

Trou aux Biches

VILLAS POINTE AUX BICHES

CALAMAR

Camp Bestel

A4

B35

Triolet

Batterie des Grenadiers

AU SOLEIL COUCHANT

Grande Pointe aux Piments

Morcellement St. André

LE VICTORIA

Black River

Solitude

Pte. aux Piments

HYATT REGENCY

20° 05'S   Baie aux Tortues or de l'Arsenal

Balaclava

MARITIM

Citrons

B41

A4

B18

The popular dive sites in the Northwest subregion are:

CARAVELLE

★★★

Location: Outside the barrier reef, opposite the Trou aux Biches Hotel. See map.
Access: By boat from all of the dive centres operating in the subregion.
Conditions: Diving conditions are normally good, with visibility varying between 25 and 30m (82-98ft). However the area is subject to tidal currents which can become strong at certain times during the month.
Average depth: 26m (85ft)
Maximum depth: 30m (98ft)

The dive site is centred on a rocky formation. Many small caves and tunnels have been created by large rocks that are piled up one on top of the other, making a torch necessary for maximum visual benefit. Flat corals grow on the rocks in shallower water, but none in deeper water. The tropical fish life is lively, comprising a variety of angelfish, batfish, soldierfish and squirrelfish. Large trumpetfish (*Aulostomus chinensis*) in their different cloaks of colour are seen on most dives, and occasionally Pineapplefish (*Cleidopus gloriamaris*) make an appearance. Large shoals of Blacktongue unicornfish (*Naso hexacanthus*) gather in the area. Barracuda pass by from time to time, as do Spotted eagle-rays (*Aetobatus narinari*). In summer White-tip sharks (*Triaenodon obesus*) are a fairly common sight and sometimes even Hammerhead (*Sphyrna* sp.) and even Tiger sharks (*Galeocerdo cuvieri*) are seen.
An occasional and spectacular visitor is the Giant reef ray (*Taeniura melanospilos*). Specimens measuring over 2m (6.6ft) and weighing over 200kg (441 lb) have been seen from time to time.

WATER LILY and *EMILY*

★★★

Location: Both wrecks are situated just south of the pass through the barrier reef, southwards of the Trou aux Biches Hotel. See map.
Access: By boat from any of the dive centres operating in the area.
Conditions: The site area is subject to tidal flow from time to time, but normally conditions are very calm. Visibility averages between 20 and 25m (66-82ft). On occasion horizontal visibility exceeds 40m (131ft).
Average depth: 23m (75ft)
Maximum depth: 26m (85ft)

Both barges, which lie about 30m (98ft) away from each other, were scuttled to make artificial reefs. While marine growth on the wrecks is moderate, a wide variety of fish life can be seen on both. A number of eels have made their homes in different corners of the rusting hulks. These include Yellow-headed moray eels (*Gymnothorax rueppelliae*), Yellow-edged (*G. flavimarginatus*) and Undulated moray eels (*G. undulatus*). Shoals of fusiliers (including *Caesio suevica* and *C. xanthonota*) add colour to the area, as do Powderblue surgeonfish (*Acanthurus leucosternon*), Moorish idols (*Zanclus canescens*) and occasionally Clown triggerfish (*Balistoides conspicillum*). Kingfish (*Caranx melampygus* and *C. sexfasciatus*) are regular visitors to the site, as is the Talang queenfish (*Scomberoides commersonianus*). Raggy and Tassled scorpionfish (*Scorpaenopsis verrucosa* and *S. oxycephala*) wait patiently for their prey and can be seen on most dives. Common stonefish (*Synanceia verrucosa*) are present on both wrecks, and so care should be taken at all times.

STELLA MARU

★★★★

Location: The ship is situated outside the reef, some 1.5km (1 mile) west of Trou aux Biches, opposite the Hotel.
Access: By boat from all of the diving centres operating in the area.
Conditions: Visibility is good, seldom below 30m (98ft). The dive site is not subject to strong currents and it is good for wide-angle photography.
Average depth: 23m (75ft)
Maximum depth: 26m (85ft)

A Japanese trawler that was purposely sunk in December 1987 by the Mauritius Marine Conservation Society, the *Stella Maru* is lying on its starboard side on a sandy floor that is dotted with flat coral patches. Although the ship has been lying underwater for over seven years there is remarkably little sea growth on it. Apart from algae, small soft corals and other marine organisms that soon cover all metallic objects underwater, there are a few anemones, spiky sea urchins and very little else. The real attraction of this dive lies, firstly, in the spectacular sight of a ship lying, still virtually intact, on the floor of the ocean. Few could deny the sense of drama one feels when seeing a ship looming ahead in the sea as you descend into the deep, gloomy water. At first it appears to be an amorphous blob that could be another patch of reef; but then, as you draw closer, that blob gradually assumes the firm and familiar shape of a ship. When you eventually reach the hulk lying on its side, drama turns to curiosity and all the time there is a sense of poignancy as one looks at the mound of broken metal that was once an integral and dynamic part of many peoples' lives and which now lies prostrate and impotent before you.

The second attraction of this dive is the interesting but subtle sea life that surrounds the ship. There are a number of small, dangerous creatures which lurk unseen to the uninitiated, either in hidden corners of the wreck or in crevices and recesses in the coral patches surrounding it. Sometimes they lie, ominously hidden just below the surface of the sand, with only their eyes showing. Angler fish (*Antennarius* sp.) and large stonefish, for example, are relatively common on the wreck, while across the sands of the sea's floor the gentle tracks of the Dragon scorpionfish or Indian walkman (*Inimicus filamentosus*) can be traced to where these perfectly camouflaged fish lurk, waiting for their prey. If you should come too close, the fish spreads its beautiful butterfly wings and the diver is treated to a display of colour and form that is an absolute privilege to witness.

In the cracks of the low coral reefs it is possible to find Spotted morays (*Gymnothorax meleagris*) and the aggressive Green moray (*Gymnothorax undulatus*). Although wreck diving is not everyone's cup of tea, it is the combination of drama and the sight of the fascinating fish life surrounding the ship's remains that makes this a highly recommended dive site. To benefit the most from the attractions this site has to offer, however, it is essential that you dive with a divemaster who knows the wreck and its marine life and who takes the trouble to show it to you.

4 ANEMONE

★★

Location: On the seaward side of the barrier reef, opposite the Trou aux Biches Hotel. See map.
Access: By boat from any of the diving centres operating in the area.
Conditions: Very light tidal current that increases during the new moon period.
Average depth: 18m (59ft)
Maximum depth: 20m (66ft)

The Stella Maru, *an artificial reef sunk in the 1980s, has remarkably little marine growth on it.*

The dive site comprises a large, flat reef with small stands of coral and patches of anemones with their attendant clownfish, or anenomefish.

The site has a diverse tropical fish population, a noticeable feature of which are the schools of goldies (*Anthias* sp.) that are seen there. The site is often used for pass-out dives for beginners and as a refresher dive site for divers who have become a little rusty.

5 THREE ANCHOR

★★

Location: On the seaward side of the reef, approximately 1km (half a mile) from the beach, opposite the PLM Azur Hotel at Mont Choisy.
Access: By boat from the diving centres in the subregion.
Conditions: There is a slight current that washes through the site area from time to time. Visibility generally averages between 15 and 20m (50-65ft).
Average depth: 16m (52ft)
Maximum depth: 21m (69ft)

The dive begins at 20m (66ft) and ends at 12m (39ft). The main attractions are three anchors from ships of the early to late 19th century. Fish and coral life in the area is meagre, but a lot of old, interesting shells and living molluscs can be seen here.

UNDERWATER WALK

Some divers may have friends with them who are not qualified divers, but still wish to experience the thrill of an underwater adventure. They have the opportunity to do so by going for a walk on the sea bed at Grand Baie! Some years ago a diving helmet with large windows allowing 180 degree viewing, was developed. The helmet is not attached to a suit, but fits over the head of the 'undersea walker' and rests on the person's shoulders. Fresh air is pumped constantly into the helmet from a compressor on the surface. Because of the balancing air pressure in the helmet, no water is able to enter it. It is not necessary for participants to be able to swim, as the object is to *walk* on the floor of the sea. Each person is given weighted anklet boots and a weight belt so that they do not find themselves lifting off the sea's floor, thus unable to walk. This sensational experience can be likened to walking on the moon, and offers participants the opportunity to enjoy a first-hand view of life on the sea bed. Book in advance at tel: 423-8822 or 263-7819/7820.

6 MANON'S CANYON

★★★

Location: The dive site is situated on the seaward side of the barrier reef off Batterie Grenadier, between Trou aux Biches and Pointe aux Piments. See map.
Access: By boat from most diving centres operating in the subregion.
Conditions: Normally very calm, occasionally subject to tidal currents, depending on the time of the month. Visibility 20-25m (66-82ft).
Average depth: 7m (23ft)
Maximum depth: 12m (39ft)

The dive site comprises a small but attractive reef patch that has both hard and soft corals and a variety of tropical fish including Red soldierfish (*Myripristis murdjan*) and Squirrelfish (*Sargocentron* sp.). The site is normally good for both macro- and wide-angle photography.

This raggy scorpionfish is almost invisible against the brightly coloured coral background.

Unlicensed shell selling is no longer permitted in Mauritius.

With the dramatic increase in tourism to Mauritius a great strain has been placed on the resources of the island, including its shells and coral.

Shell buying by tourists from local vendors has resulted in an unsustainable collecting of shells in order to generate income for those unable to obtain employment in the formal sector, but the result has caused an imbalance in a once-rich ecological heritage, which is being plundered and rapidly rendered useless for future generations.

While the need for the poor and unemployed to earn an income is understandable, it is of little avail in the long term if the island's rich heritage is destroyed.

Sadly, too, turtles are rare visitors to Mauritian shores as their shells, once plentiful, have been exploited by the poor and sold to the rich. Indeed, the poor are now worse off as the sea returns less and less for greater effort!

The Mauritian government has done much to find other ways of employing the masses; to this end it has gone a long way in establishing industries and formal employment opportunities on the island. It is assuring that the sale of shells, coral and turtle shell has been banned. Regrettably though, this ban doesn't appear to have been taken very seriously as these particular items are boldly displayed and sold in souvenir emporia, gift shops and occasionally by furtive beach vendors.

When questioned, shopkeepers will deny they come from Mauritius, asserting that they have been imported from countries elsewhere in the Indian Ocean and from the Far East. Nevertheless, one is never certain whether it is the truth. There is also not much logic to the practice: every species taken from the sea, irrespective of where it is taken from, contributes to its eventual extinction – unless it is done on a controlled and sustainable basis, which, unfortunately, is not the case at present.

It should be noted that tourists who do not have a valid permit for the possession and transport of marine species are also guilty of an offence and liable to prosecution as well as to the confiscation of the specimens on leaving Mauritius. Even if you were able to avoid the Mauritian customs authorities, you could face problems on returning home, especially if you come from a country which has signed agreements on endangered species.

Illegal possession of marine specimens can result in prosecution and confiscation at home, so it is better not to take the chance.

7 ANCHOR HOLE
also known as LOST ANCHOR

★★★

Location: On the seaward side of the barrier reef, opposite Club Meditérranée. See map.
Access: Through most of the diving centres operating in the area.
Conditions: Normally conditions are calm, but occasionally there is a gentle tidal current. Visibility averages between 20 and 25m (66-82ft).
Average depth: 22m (72ft)
Maximum depth: 31m (102ft)

The dive site comprises a small reef patch which ascends from a depth of 31m (102ft) upwards to 22m (72ft), at the top of which there is a hole containing a 17th century anchor. The origin of this anchor remains a mystery. The dive site has a limited variety of hard and soft corals and gorgonians, including some picturesque sea fans.

8 STENOPUS REEF

★★★★

Location: Situated on the seaward side of the barrier reef, just south of Pointe aux Canonniers. See map.
Access: By boat from any of the diving centres operating in the subregion.
Conditions: Visibility usually ranges between 20 and 30m (66-98ft), but reaches more than 40m (131ft) from time to time.
Average depth: 29m (95ft)
Maximum depth: 38m (125ft)

The dive starts at 38m (125ft) and ends at 11m (36ft). It is a very picturesque dive site containing many interesting features, such as tubastrea corals of more than 2m (7ft) in height. There are large fan corals which decorate the walls of the drop-off, and a wide variety of soft corals add a subtle hue. Another interesting aspect of the dive is that, while it has a large number and a wide variety of

The pretty Mauritian boxfishes usually swim in a small group; this one has strayed from the school.

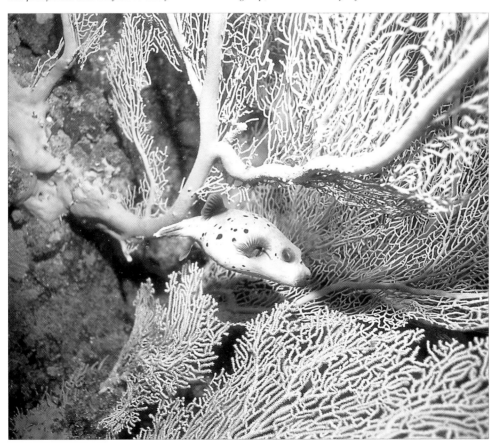

A shallow dive allows plenty of natural light on Mauritius's softly coloured corals.

tropical fish, many pelagic fish species can also be seen here because of the site's exposure to the deep waters of the open sea. Kingfish, wahoo, stingrays and tuna are frequent visitors to the dive site. Sometimes White-tip reef sharks (*Triaenodon obesus*) are seen and occasionally dolphin make a brief appearance. It is the combination of the site's fauna and flora that makes this dive a highly recommended one.

9 PETER HOLT'S ROCK
also known as THE BOULDERS

★★★

Location: South of Pointe aux Canonniers. See map.
Access: By boat from any of the diving centres operating in this subregion.

Conditions: Occasionally there is a slight current which creates conditions more suitable for a drift dive. Visibility averages from 20-25m (66-82ft), but sometimes reaches 35-40m (115-131ft).
Average depth: 18m (59ft)
Maximum depth: 21m (69ft)

Huge basalt rocks of volcanic origin, some larger than an average-sized Mauritian house, form the dominant landscape feature of this dive site. Between the rocks are caves, tunnels, cracks and crevices, and in almost every one is some form of interesting marine life; there is much to explore during the dive. The most common resident is crayfish (lobster). There are lots of fan corals and soft corals on the rocks and a wide variety of porcupinefish (*Diodon histrix, D. holocanthus, Cyclichthys antennatus*), and Bigeye emperor fish (*Monotaxis grandoculus*) often swim among them, while Giant moray eels (*Gymnothorax javanicus*) are seen on most dives.

DIVING COSTS

The cost of dives in the subregion varies from Rs350 to Rs600 a dive.

DIVING CENTRES

Dive centres operating in this region are:

• Nautilus Diving Centre,
Le Trou aux Biches Hotel.
Tel: 261-6562 Fax: 261-6611

This dive centre operates from premises at the Trou aux Biches Hotel. It has 20 complete sets of equipment for hire (Scubapro and Cressi-Sub); diving cylinders are either 12- or 15-litre steel. The centre operates two boats: 21ft and 23ft broad-beam flat-bottomed monohulls powered by twin 25HP motors. Nautilus is a registered member of the Mauritian Scuba Diving Association (MSDA) and is affiliated to both CMAS and DIWA. Training is offered from a basic introductory course to Divemaster.

• Blue Water Diving Centre,
Le Corsaire, Trou aux Biches.
Tel: 261-5209 Fax: 261-6267

Blue Water Diving Centre operates from the premises of Corsaire Angling Club in Trou aux Biches.

The centre offers general diving to the public. It also offers specialized diving for advanced divers, marine biologists, underwater photographers and underwater film-makers.

Blue Water Diving has equipment to kit out 15 divers, complete with all the necessary gear. It has 40 (mainly steel) tanks of different capacities, including 9-, 10-, 12- and 15-litres.

The centre has three boats: a 28ft cabin cruiser powered by a 145HP inboard motor plus an auxiliary outboard motor; a twin-hull 25ft fibreglass boat powered by twin 40HP motors; and a small wooden 21ft boat powered by twin 25HP motors.

Training is offered, from a beginner's introductory course to CMAS Three-Star (Assistant Instructor) certification. (Three months' prior notification is required in order to arrange for special examiners from overseas.) Blue Water Diving is a registered member of MSDA.

• Paradise Diving Centre,
PLM Azur Hotel, Mont Choisy,
Trou aux Biches.
Tel: 261-6970 Fax: 261-6749
or Tel: 263-7220 Fax: 263-8534

This is a division of Paradise Diving which is based in Grand Baie. (For more details see the relevant section on Paradise Diving [page 95]).

• Turtle Bay Nautics
(Maritim Diving Centre), Maritim Hotel,
Balaclava, Terre Rouge.
Tel: 261-5600 Fax 261-5670

Turtle Bay Nautics (which is also known as Maritim Diving Centre) operates from the Maritim Hotel at Balaclava, north of Port Louis. The centre has a full range of equipment and is capable of kitting out 10 divers. It operates a 20ft Tremlett monohull, powered by twin 40HP motors. The centre is affiliated to CMAS and offers training from an introductory course to Two-Star certification. It is a registered member of MSDA. In addition to using the dive sites described in this subregion, the centre takes its clients to six of its own sites situated closer to its place of operation.

• Diving World,
Hotel Le Canonnier,
Pointe aux Cannoniers.
Tel: 263-7999 Fax: 263-7864

This dive centre, at Hotel Le Canonnier, only recently began an independent operation. It has Scubapro equipment and can kit out nine divers. The centre has a Tremlett 27x8ft fibreglass boat which is powered by twin 90HP motors.

The centre is affiliated to NAUI and offers training from a basic introductory course to Open Water One certification.

PLACES OF INTEREST

Aquarium
The Aquarium Centre has been established on the coastal road through Trou aux Biches near the turnoff to Triolet. Here it is possible to see a variety of fascinating marine creatures which inhabit some of Mauritius's underwater wonderland. Open Mon-Sat (09:00-17:00) and Sun (09:00-16:00).

SPORT AND RECREATIONAL ACTIVITIES

Watersports
Water-skiing, windsurfing, yachting, riding in a *pedalo*, parasailing and trips in a fibreglass-bottomed boat are offered by most hotels.

Facilities are usually available to nonresidents at some hotels, and enquiries should be made at the reception or at the hotel's boathouse.

Deep-sea fishing
Mauritius is world-renowned for marlin fishing. The best months for deep-sea fishing are October to March. Trips can be arranged through reception for hotel guests, and nonresidents can make arrangements with:

Organisation de Pêche du Nord (Corsaire Club), Royal Road,
Trou aux Biches.
Tel: 261-6264 Fax: 261-6611

Horseracing
The Champ de Mars, oldest race track in the southern hemisphere, is cradled in the Moka mountains on the eastern side of Port Louis. It was a military parade ground in the days of the French, and in 1812, shortly after the British took over the administration of the island, it was converted to a horseracing track and the Mauritian Turf Club was formed. Meetings are held there every Saturday afternoon from the first week in May to the end of November.

EATING OUT

Most hotels in this subregion structure their tariffs on a dinner, bed and breakfast basis, and most have restaurants which also cater for the general public, for example, **La Coquille**, situated at Casuarina Village, **Le Frangipanier** and **Le Navigator** at **Le Canonnier Hotel**, **Le Barachois** and **Le Wahoo** at the PLM Azur Hotel. In addition there are a number of independent restaurants which offer an interesting variety of cuisine: **L'Exotique**, which serves Creole and European food; **Le Lagoon Blue**, which offers grilled seafood as a speciality; and **Le Sireue Restaurant** concentrates on seafood and Indian dishes.

In the translucent waters of Mauritius there is almost no chance of bumping into the dreaded man-eating sharks that movies are made of. That is not to say, however, that sharks are not found here. They are, and the sighting of one while diving is a definite highlight, provided the shark is accorded due respect.

The most common sharks which divers are likely to encounter in Mauritius are the Black-tip reef shark, the White-tip reef shark and the Grey reef shark.

Less frequent visitors to the island are Sicklefin lemon sharks, Sandbar sharks, Silver-tip sharks, Tiger sharks, Whale sharks, awkward-looking Great hammerheads, Zambezi or Bull sharks, Dusky sharks and Ragged-tooth sharks.

The last three mentioned are very infrequent visitors to Mauritian waters. In the open sea that lies beyond the island's reefs, a number of pelagic shark species comb the sea looking for prey. The only people likely to encounter these are big-game fishermen who seek them out as a challenge to their skill and a stimulant for their adrenalin. Here the main shark species comprise the Oceanic white-tip shark (*Carcharhinus longimanus*), the fearsome Great white shark (*Carcharodon carcharias*), the Mako shark (*Isurus oxyrinchus*) and the Blue shark (*Prionace glauca*).

Black-tip Reef Shark
(*Carcharhinus melanopterus*)

The **Black-tip reef shark** is the most common shark in Mauritian waters and is found throughout the tropical areas of the Indo-Pacific region. It is the smallest shark found around the island, seldom reaching more than 1.6m (5ft) in length. Aptly named for the prominent black blotches on the tips of all but the anal fin, the Black-tip reef shark's body is generally pale brown or beige in colour. A white band runs along the flank from the anal fin to below the first dorsal fin. The fish's snout is rounded, even blunt, and so gives the impression of not being as streamlined as that of some of its cousins, but don't be misled by this: these sharks are swift and strong swimmers!

Black-tip reef sharks often come in close to the shore and can be seen patrolling shallow reefs within the intertidal zone looking for invertebrates and small fishes to eat. Sometimes their diet stretches to much bigger fishes such as kingfish and even large groupers. Juveniles often come into the lagoons where life is a little safer and quieter, but the adults tend to prefer the deeper waters of the drop-off on the outer reef. They are often seen alone, but they also gather in small groups and there are occasions when as many as 30 have been seen together. It is at these times that care should be taken, as they can become aggressive and have been known to attack human beings – probably mistaking them for prey. Particular care should be taken when there are spearfishermen and speared fish in the area. Sightings of Black-tip reef fish are most common at Casiers and Passe St Jacques in the Southwest subregion.

White-tip Reef Shark
(*Triaenodon obesus*)

The **White-tip reef shark** is slender and greyish-brown with prominent white tips on its first dorsal and upper caudal fins, as well as on the upper lobe of the tail fin. There is no ridge between the dorsal fins. The shark has a very broad snout with ridges on its brow which gives it an almost quizzical look. Its preferred food is small fish, octopus, eels and crustaceans. The White-tip reef shark is often seen in clear shallow water on reef flats and sometimes in deeper water on the drop-off. However, the most common sightings are made while the shark is resting in a crevice, in a cave or under an overhang. It is harmless and shy, preferring to avoid confrontation, but, as with all animals in Nature, it will become aggressive if it is provoked or feels trapped.

Grey reef sharks are a common sight in Mauritius, and are usually very docile.

Grey Reef Sharks
(*Carcharhinus amblyrhynchos*)

The **Grey reef shark** is the one to watch out for, but fortunately when it is feeling crotchety, it lets you know! It arches its back, drops its pectoral fins and swims erratically. Don't stop to watch its antics or to wonder why it is behaving like this – just quietly and quickly get out of the water! Normally Grey reef sharks are docile and well behaved but they have a short fuse and can become agitated very quickly. The trick is not to provoke the shark and not to become unnerved when a group of them comes to within a metre of you to find out who and what you are. They are very inquisitive, but will leave you in peace once they have satisfied their curiosity and you have to let them do this in a way that neither threatens them nor conveys any fear you may be feeling. Grey reef sharks are common in Mauritius. They are coastal, inshore sharks which inhabit fringe reefs and deeper banks and can be found at the surface and intertidal zone, but also at depths of 140m (459ft) and more.

Juveniles prefer shallow water and are frequently found on reef flats. These sharks seem to prefer the leeward (western) side of the island and often congregate in areas where there are strong currents, usually keeping on or at least very near to the bottom of the reefs.

The Grey reef shark is also known by some as the **Black-tail reef shark**, as the broad black band along the rear edge of the tail-fin is a typical feature of this fish. Other distinctive markings are the black tips of the pectoral fins and the fact that the second dorsal fin, the anal fin and the pelvic fin are all black. The shark has a long, somewhat rounded snout, serrated teeth and a stocky body. It varies in size from 1.2 to 1.5m (4–5ft) but some have reportedly measured as long as 2.3m (8ft).

Found in clear, shallow water, the White-tip reef shark is usually a shy fish.

Sicklefin Lemon Sharks
(Negaprion acutidens)

Sicklefin lemon sharks are not that common in Mauritius. They are usually found on the bed of the sea, swimming slowly or resting on the sand. The shark is a pale, yellowish-brown in colour and has a large stocky body with a short snout. Its dorsal fins are virtually equal in size. Juveniles are seldom seen in deep waters; they tend to stick to shallow reef flats where they can be seen swimming about with both dorsal fins often breaking the surface of the sea.

Mature Sicklefins are usually about 2m (7ft) in length, although the records indicate that specimens exceeding 3m (10ft) have been observed. They feed on bottom-dwelling bony fishes. These sharks are shy and elusive and tend to avoid divers, but they do have a reputation for becoming very aggressive when provoked and there have been instances where they have made unprovoked attacks on divers. The golden rule applies: be careful and don't panic.

Silver-tip Sharks
(Carcharhinus albimarginatus)

Silver-tip sharks reach lengths in excess of 3m (10ft). They are easily recognizable by the white (silver) tips on both the upper and lower lobes of their tails, as well as on their dorsal and pectoral fins.

These sharks are both coastal (they swim close to the shore) and pelagic (they live in deeper waters) and so frequent the surface of the sea as well as depths estimated to be in excess of 600m (1969ft).

They are also found in lagoons, along the reefs and on the drop-offs.

Silver-tip sharks breed in Mauritian waters during the months of December and January, at Gunner's Quoin, Round Island and Flat Island – all off the northern tip of the main island. Pregnant females usually drop between five and six pups. This ubiquitous shark feeds on a wide range of prey – from flying fish to midwater and bottom-dwelling fish such as tuna, wahoo, kingfish, rays, soles and octopus.

Sandbar Shark
(Carcharhinus plumbeus)

It may seem ironical but the distinguishing feature of the **Sandbar shark** is that it has little that is distinctive: the high, triangular-shaped dorsal fin is perhaps its only outstanding feature. It has a stocky and short, rounded snout with large, triangular-shaped, serrated teeth. It feeds on a wide variety of fish, octopus, shrimp and crabs. Mature Sandbar sharks may reach 2.3m (8ft) in length, but in Mauritian waters they seldom grow longer than 1.8m (6ft).

These fish tend to avoid sandy beaches and the surf zone. Usually solitary swimmers, they also congregate at times into packs. When alone they tend to be shy, but in a pack can become very inquisitive.

The Oceanic White-tip Shark
(Carcharhinus longimanus)

The **Oceanic white-tip shark** is a large, stocky creature with distinctive paddle-shaped pectoral fins which are white-tipped. It is not a frequent visitor to Mauritian waters. Generally this shark prefers deep open water and is seldom seen at depths shallower than 40m (131ft).

However, it can occasionally be seen swimming leisurely just below the surface of the sea. Don't be fooled by its apparent docility; it is known to become very aggressive. An inquisitive shark whose curiosity is not easily satisfied, its persistent interest can become disquieting. Many attacks on shipwrecked people have been attributed to the Oceanic white-tip shark and it is, therefore, worth avoiding.

This particular shark has a grey-bronze upper body with a white underside, and large broad teeth which are deeply serrated. Seabirds, pelagic fish, sardines, octopus, squid, turtles and even garbage form part of its diet. Usually about 1.7m (5.6ft) long at maturity, some specimens measuring 3m (10ft) have been recorded.

Great Hammerhead
(Sphyrna mokarran and *S. zygaena)*

This shark is easily distinguished by its large flattened head which extends in width past either side of its body. The species is the largest of the hammerhead family and reaches up to 3.5m (12ft) in length. The **Great hammerhead** has a dark grey or brown back with a high dorsal fin, and a white belly. In Mauritian waters it is usually seen offshore around Gunner's Quoin, Round Island and Flat Island, and occasionally off the Le Morne peninsula at Casiers. Hammerheads are nomads and cover great distances, patrolling the sea from the surface to great depths in search of food.

Blue Shark
(Prionace glauca)

A beautiful fish with bright blue flanks, a dark blue back and a white belly, the Blue shark is also a graceful swimmer. It has a large slender body with long, thin pectoral fins and a long and pointed snout. This streamlining not only gives the shark great speed, but also a sense of elegance and efficiency as it swiftly glides past in the water.

The Blue shark is a surface-feeder and preys primarily on smaller sharks, sea birds, shoaling fish and squid. It is known to venture close inshore at night.

Although there are no recorded attacks by Blue sharks on divers, they are inquisitive and often come in close to see who the intruders are. Spearfishermen consider them a nuisance. The International Game Fishing Association's world record for a Blue shark weighing 183.6kg (405 lb) was landed in Mauritius.

Whale Shark
(Rhincodon typus)

Surely the gentle giant of the ocean, the **Whale shark**, huge and daunting in appearance, is actually harmless. It tolerates divers

The world's largest fish, Whale sharks feed on plankton as do baleen whales.

hitching a lift by holding onto its dorsal fin or by hanging onto its lips. It is the world's largest living fish, reaching 18m (59ft) in length, and weighing up to 18 tonnes! It feeds on plankton and small fish which it filters through its large, cavernous mouth. Only occasionally seen in Mauritius, little is known about its life cycle.

Tiger Shark
(*Galeocerdo cuvieri*)

A voracious predator on fishes, birds, mammals and turtles, the **Tiger shark** has been implicated in attacks on humans along the African coast. No attacks have been recorded in Mauritian waters. It reaches 5.5m (18ft) in length and weighs up to 560kg (1235 lb). It is sexually mature at 3m (10ft). The shark has large, saw-edged cockscomb teeth that are capable of cutting through bone and flesh like a hot knife through butter. This is one shark you don't hitch a ride on – keep a very wary eye on it and rather

abort your dive, without any evidence of panic, if it shows any signs of interest in you. Discretion *is* the better part of valour!

Mako Shark
(*Isurus oxyrinchus*)

The **Mako shark** grows to a maximum length of 4m (13ft), and has a brilliant blue back. An open water shark, it is seldom seen in reef waters. It feeds on game fish, smaller sharks and squid, and relies on speed and manoeuvrability to catch its prey. At full run Mako sharks have been estimated to reach unbelievable speeds of up to 60kph (37mph), making them a game fisherman's dream to catch!

Great White Shark
(*Carcharodon carcharias*)

A notorious denizen of the deep, the **Great white shark** is, fortunately, a rare visitor to Mauritian waters. Adults prefer to hunt in the cooler seas of temperate regions, while juveniles are more often seen in warm, sub-tropical waters. Great whites are easy to confuse with Mako sharks, but if you are unlucky to get close enough you may notice that its teeth are more serrated! Fortunately, the chance of seeing a Great white around Mauritius is very remote indeed.

Zambezi or Bull shark
(*Carcharhinus leucas*)

This shark is circumglobal and is usually found in estuaries, on occasion many miles upstream where the waters are no longer salty, so is seldom seen in Mauritian waters. The **Zambezi or Bull shark**,is dangerous and must be treated with extreme caution. It is a robust grey creature with a high dorsal fin and broad, triangular-shaped, saw-edged upper teeth. It has no distinctive markings. Its principal foods are small sharks, fishes and dolphins.

Dusky Shark
(*Carcharhinus obscurus*)

The **Dusky shark** occurs worldwide. It has a small front dorsal fin and its back dorsal fin is very low. It is dusky grey in colour, hence its name. The shark's principal foods are fish and squid. This fish grows up to 4.2m (14ft) in length and the heaviest specimen on record weighed 327kg (721 lb). It is an infrequent visitor to Mauritian waters.

Ragged-tooth Shark
(*Carcharias taurus*)

Ragged-tooth sharks are greyish-brown in colour, but in certain light they appear to be a dull silver, with small, dark brown spots along their sides. Their dorsal and anal fins are equal in size. A most fearsome-looking creature with rows of ragged teeth, it has a placid temperament and only becomes dangerous if provoked. Only very infrequently seen in Mauritian waters.

POINTERS IN BEHAVIOUR TOWARDS SHARKS

• Treat all sharks with absolute respect. While some are harmless and docile, others are not – don't rely on your ability to distinguish between them!

• Don't dive with an open wound or where fishermen are cleaning their catches.

• Avoid dirty water with poor visibility. Not only does this impair your vision but sharks are attracted to this sort of water to feed.

• Always dive with a buddy and stay close together.

• Be careful at dusk, when sharks are known to be particularly active.

• If sharks become very inquisitive and bold it is better to get out of the water, even if your nerves can stand it. If possible keep your back against the rocks and go to the surface back-to-back with your buddy.

• Be calm, particularly in your movements! A shark may mistake quick movements for those of a struggling fish and an easy meal. Remember, sharks have poor eyesight and are attracted by movement and smell. Make sure you don't splash unnecessarily in case the shark should mistake you for a fish or a creature in distress.

• Should you fail to allay the shark's attention, remember that its snout is sensitive and a sharp blow to it with a knife or shark billy is likely to dampen its ardour. But be extremely careful, it could make the shark even more aggressive, so only use this tactic as a last resort!

• Relax! The likelihood of a shark being more than just a little curious is slim and the chance of you getting hurt is far greater in your journey getting to and from the dive site than it is in the water.

THE NORTH

This subregion stretches from Pointe aux Canonniers in the west to Grand Gaube in the east and includes the offshore islands of Coin de Mire, Flat Island with its sister island Gabriel Island, Round Island and Serpent Island. The North is, in many ways, the focal point for tourism in Mauritius. Because the area is sheltered from the prevailing winds from the southeast and offers easy access to a variety of beaches in both the north and the northwest, it has many tourist attractions. Grand Baie has grown from a sleepy holiday village to a tourist town comprising a medley of shops, restaurants and hotels and a number of night-clubs. The bay itself is not particularly well suited to swimming, except along its northern shores where a number of major hotel developments have taken place. There is no diving in the bay as it is too shallow, but it provides access to the reefs that lie beyond. It is very popular for sailing, windsurfing and water-skiing. To the east of Grand Baie is Péreybère which is both a residential and a resort area. Here there are a number of small hotels, guesthouses and villas to let, so it is popular with lower budget and self-catering tourists. Further east is Cap Malheureux, which is the most northerly point of Mauritius. Here, at the place where a Catholic church stands today, the English army landed in 1810 in its successful invasion of the island. To the east of Cap Malheureux is Grand Gaube, the boundary between the northern and the eastern subregions.

Coin de Mire (or Gunner's Quoin as the English called it) stands proudly on the horizon of a flat sea. The island gained its name from its wedge shape, which resembles the wedges that ship's gunners used to raise the angle of their cannon's barrel and to steady their aim. The island was used in the past as a military post and quarantine area for boats arriving with crews carrying contagious diseases. Ile Ronde (Round Island) and Ile aux Serpent (Snake Island) lie about 24km (15 miles) offshore and are nature reserves. Ile Ronde is only 151ha (373 acres) in extent but it is home to a great number of endangered species which have been able to survive through the centuries because of the lack of human interference.

Left: Coin de Mire, or Gunner's Quoin, is so-named because its shape resembles the wedge used by gunners to steady their cannons when firing. Above: *Semicircular angelfish occur in coastal reefs with heavy coral growth.*

DIVING CONDITIONS

The offshore islands are linked to the main island by an undersea platform that seldom reaches a depth greater than 50m (164ft) and the sharp drop-off, characteristic of volcanic islands, only occurs some distance beyond the dive sites. The effect of this extensive, relatively shallow shelf means that this subregion is largely protected from the influences of the open sea, and this, combined with the protection from the prevailing southeast winds afforded by the land, means that the subregion can offer protected year-round diving. Water temperatures vary from 26–28°C (79–82°F) in summer to 20–24°C (68–75°F) in winter.

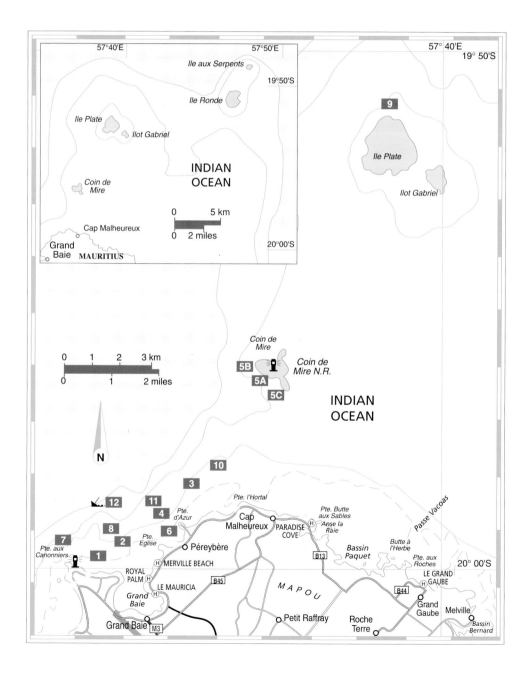

Popular dive sites in the North sub-region are:

AQUARIUM
also known as WEST REEF

★★★★

Location: The dive is situated just left of the exit from the Grand Baie barrier reef pass. See map.
Access: Access to the site is by boat from any of the dive centres operating in the region, and takes between 10 and 20 minutes to reach, depending on point of departure. The dive site is used by all diving centres operating in the North and Northwest subregions.
Conditions: Visibility is good, averaging between 20 and 30m (66-98ft), but in ideal conditions it sometimes exceeds 50m (164ft). There is a slight tidal current before new and full moon.
Average depth: 10m (33ft)
Maximum depth: 15m (49ft)

This site is aptly named for the wide variety of fish life that can be found here.

Typical fish that can be seen in reasonable numbers are wrasses, butterflyfish (Chataedons), angelfish, various species of surgeonfish including many highly decorative Moorish idols (Zanclus canescens), soldierfish, sweetlips and anemonefish.

Also present is the aggressive Green moray eel (Gymnothorax undulatus).

A number of scorpionfish, particularly the Hump-backed scorpionfish (Scorpaenopsis gibbosa), can also be seen, while Devil firefish (Pterois miles) decorate the site with their delicate, but dangerous feathers.

Care must also be taken not to touch the Angler fish (Antennarius sp.) or the stonefish (Synanceia verrucosa), which have poisonous spikes along their backs.

This site is perfect for night diving, and plays host to Spanish dancers (Hexabranchus sanguineus) that flap their bright red skirts to the rhythm of the sea, and add colour and beauty to the dive. Remember to take a torch along on the dive, so that you don't miss these beauties.

SHIFTING ALLEGIANCES

Suckerfishes, such as Remoras or Shark suckers (Echeneis naucrates), have suction pads on the top of their heads which they use to attach themselves to their hosts – thereby hitching a ride to new feeding grounds. With larger hosts, such as sharks and rays, however, the suckerfish may travel independently, albeit very close to the host's skin, sometimes as near as 2-3cm (1in) away.

TORTOISE
also known as MERVILLE PATCHES, MERVILLE AQUARIUM, MONIKA REEF and MORAY REEF.

★★★★

Location: The site area is situated approximately 1.5km (1 mile) offshore and is situated just beyond the barrier reef, directly opposite the Merville Hotel. See map.
Access: Access is by boat from any one of the dive centres operating in the North (or in the Northwest). The journey takes 10-30 minutes.
Conditions: There is invariably a slight current which makes it possible to drift from one section of the dive area to the next. However, the current is not so strong that it makes it difficult to remain in one of the eight reefs which compose the total dive area for the duration of the dive.
Average depth: 12-13m (39-43ft)
Maximum depth: 13m (43ft)

The area is a breeding ground and is therefore densely populated, particularly by juvenile fish just after the egg-hatching season. Resident throughout the year is a wide variety of tropical reef fish, bringing colour and constant movement to the dive site.

Also common are stonefish (Synanceia sp.), lionfish (Pterois sp.) and scorpionfish (Scorpaenopsis sp.).

There are three resident moray eels which are often fed by divers – considered by some to be a dubious practice. And then there is dear old Monika, a large moray which has something wrong with one eye but is always happy to say 'hello' to passing divers.

The rare Rhino moray (or Ribbon eel) (Rhinomureana quasita), which can be either dark blue or black in colour, and has a yellow stripe and a long, whiskered head, has also been seen on the site. Octopus are frequently encountered, so keep an eye on likely holes and you should not be disappointed. Study the anemones closely and you may see little shrimps inhabiting them. Triggerfish are common and Madras, a local name for Blue-and-yellow sea perch (Lutjanus kasmira), often swim in the area in large shoals. This is a beautiful, bright yellow fish with cobalt blue stripes. Another interesting fish found here in the summer season, between November and May, is the Giant triggerfish (Balistoides viridescens). While brooding, the female of the species becomes very aggressive and is known to attack divers who come too close to her nest or who threaten her brood in any way.

Small hard corals occur as well as two species of plate corals, but they are beginning to show heavy signs of damage resulting partially from the increasing number of divers in the area, but more particularly from net-fishing, and the careless dropping of anchors onto the coral. This site gains four stars for its variety of fish, rather than for its corals.

⓷ CORAL GARDENS
also known as SUNJAY PATCHES

★★★

Location: The site is situated halfway between Grand Baie and Coin de Mire, approximately 1.5km (1 mile) offshore and beyond the barrier reef. See map.
Access: By boat (15-30 mins) from any one of the diving centres operating in the North and Northwest.
Conditions: Visibility is normally very good, in excess of 25m (82ft) and at times beyond 50m (164ft). A slight tidal current is normal for this dive.
Average depth: 15m (49ft)
Maximum depth: 21m (69ft)

The site is composed of banks of coral reefs interspersed with sand gullies. The corals, which include a number of soft ones, are varied, but plate corals tend to dominate and as a result the site tends to be grey in colour, making it visually boring. The coral is generally in good condition, but damage from anchors and net fishing is evident. Squirrelfish and goldies are common and trumpetfish occasionally weave their way through the site area. Crayfish can be seen in a number of crevices throughout the dive. The site has two friendly resident Giant moray eels. Turtles are seen in this area from time to time. The site makes an interesting night dive.

⓸ POINTE VACOAS,
also known as POINTE AZUR, and CORAL GARDENS

★★★★

Location: The dive site is situated about 500-600m (547-656yds) off Péreybère Reef opposite Pointe d'Azur. See map.
Access: By boat from all diving centres operating in the North and Northwest. The journey takes 15-35 minutes, depending on point of departure.
Conditions: Visibility is generally very good, usually up to 25m (82ft), but frequently up to 50m (164ft) or more. A gentle tidal current is common.
Average depth: 22m (72ft)
Maximum depth: 25m (80ft)

There are both hard and soft corals, and the hard corals often branch prettily upwards to form alleyways or overhangs between them, while an abundance of tropical fish adds colour and beauty to the site. Giant starfish (*Linckia lacrigata*), which grow up to 40cm (16in), and very large firefish are a notable feature of this site. Between August and December dolphins sometimes come to the area to play, thrilling divers with their grace and turn of speed. On occasion a 2m-long (6.6ft) Giant moray eel has been seen swimming above the reef; it has been nicknamed 'the Bandit'.

⓹ GUNNER'S QUOIN
also known as COIN DE MIRE

★★ to ★★★★ (See below)

Location: Coin de Mire is a wedge-shaped island lying approximately 6km (4 miles) north of the main island of Mauritius. There are at least 10 different dive sites around the island, but their use and suitability depends on the experience and levels of competency of the divers. See map.
Access: By boat, the journey takes between 25 and 45 minutes, depending on the point of departure.
Conditions: Tides or currents can become tricky and therefore not all of the dive centres take clients to the island; those that do only take experienced divers. The dives are usually drift dives.
Average depth: 10-20m (33-66ft)
Maximum depth: 26-40m (85-131ft)

Three dive sites are most frequently used:

A. Confetti Bay: This site is so named because of the abundance of fusilier fish, which, when the sun is overhead, sparkle in the light, giving the impression of falling confetti. This is a shallow dive with an average depth of 14m (46ft) and a maximum depth of 22m (72ft).

Sea goldies in a colony of hard corals.

Rays are a common sight on the sandy floor and there are plenty of tropical fish about. The condition of the corals is not good because of damage caused to them by the careless use of anchors and illegal net-fishing. For this reason the site has been relegated to only a two-star rating. It is a suitable site for beginners, but it is usually used as the point of entry for a drift dive to either of the two sites described below – which one depends on prevailing current direction.

B. The Wall: This spectacular dive site comprises a black rock face with a steep drop-off on which there is a variety of marine organisms, including oyster-clams and feather stars (crinoid echinoderms). Here, too, a wide variety of pelagic fish provides excitement and interest. Dogtooth tunny (*Gymnosarda unicolor*), wahoo (*Acanthocybium solandri*), various species of rays, barracuda (*Sphyraena jello*) – often in large shoals – large parrotfish, and dolphins are frequent visitors, while manta (*Manta birostris*), sailfish (*Istiophorus platypterus*), White-tip sharks (*Triaenodon obesus*) and marlin (*Makaira* sp.) have been seen in the months of November and December – usually while conditions are unsettled in the aftermath of a heavy storm.

Observing the grace and effortless ease with which these impressive creatures make their way through the water and the sense of excitement that they bring to the diver earns this site its four-star rating.

C. The Anchor: This dive is usually done as a drift dive to an old anchor, probably dating back to the 18th century. En route the diver passes through forests of gorgonians, some of which rise up to 2m (6.6ft) in height. Surgeonfish add colour and interest as they weave their way through the gorgonians, seemingly playing hide-and-seek with their human visitors. A variety of brightly coloured tropical fish, together with the symmetry and beauty of the sea fans and other soft corals, add up to making this a highly recommended site. The site offers a number of opportunities for silhouette photography.

As an alternative, and using an anchor, it can also be dived as a single site.

Coin de Mire is well known for the many birds that live there, particularly the White- and Red-tailed Tropicbirds (*Phaethon lepturus* and *P. rubricauda*). Occasionally, if the diver is very lucky, they may be seen catching their main food source – flying fish – or even taking squid out of the water.

Mauritius, as with many of the other islands in the Indian Ocean, was once a breeding ground for the marine turtle. Today, however, an encounter with a turtle while diving in Mauritian waters is a rare privilege that must be savoured.

The history of marine turtles can be traced back for at least 200 million years, and apart from sea snakes, they are the only marine reptiles that were also in existence during the days of the dinosaurs.

There are seven marine turtle species, all of which are on the endangered species list. Five are found in Mauritian and southern Indian Ocean waters, four of which belong to the same family, Cheloniidae. These are the Loggerhead (*Caretta caretta*), the Olive Ridley (*Lepidochelys olivacea*), the Green (*Chelonia mydas*) and the Hawksbill (*Eretmochelys imbricata*) turtles. The remaining species, the Leatherback turtle (*Dermochelys coriacea*), is the sole survivor of the family Dermochelidae. Both families are of the suborder Cryptodira.

This Green turtle, after laying her eggs, will return to the sea, leaving her hatchlings to fend for themselves.

Turtles vary in size. The largest are the Leatherbacks which grow to a length of between 2.5 and 3m (8–10ft) and weigh, in some cases, in excess of 900kg (1985 lb). Green turtles vary in length from 1.2–1.5m (4–5ft), with a maximum mass of 275kg (606 lb). Loggerhead turtles are slightly smaller, between 1 and 1.2m (3–4ft) with a mass of 160kg (353lb). Hawksbill turtles seldom reach more than 1m (3ft) in length and have a maximum mass of 135kg (298 lb), while the Olive Ridley is the smallest, with a maximum length of 85cm (33in) and a mass of 46kg (101 lb).

The nesting habits of turtles make a fascinating story. Once gravid, research has revealed that turtles return to the nesting beaches where they themselves were hatched despite the many thousands of kilometres they will have travelled since birth.

This astounding ability to cross open oceans, travel vast distances – all of it done underwater in an environment where celestial navigational aids are not available – and to return to the beaches on which they were hatched is one of Nature's best kept secrets: their homing ability requires highly evolved guidance mechanisms which, despite extensive research, are not yet scientifically understood.

Nesting, which is done mainly at night, is a slow and laborious process and lasts for at least an hour. At high tide, the gravid female emerges from the sea and rests in the wash zone of the beach. Once satisfied that there is no danger, she advances up the beach in order to find a suitable site to lay her eggs. Here she digs herself in using her fore-flippers. Once settled, she carefully digs an egg cavity with her rear flippers to a depth of between 25 and 45cm (10–18 inch) into which, after a short rest, she lays her eggs and then returns to the sea.

Between 50 and 70 days later, the hatchlings emerge from their nest in the sand. Once on the surface of the beach, each matchbox-sized hatchling faces the formidable task of finding the sea, which might be

It is a special sight indeed to encounter a marine turtle.

a few hundred metres away. The run to the sea is a time of great risk as the hatchlings are exposed to many dangers – the predations of ghost crabs, monitor lizards and birds, or dehydration from the sun if they don't reach the sea before sunrise.

Mauritius was once a breeding ground for Loggerhead, Green and Hawksbill turtles. But the meat and oil from the livers of

Turtles are an endangered species and should not be interfered with in any way.

these tortoises of the sea made them highly sought after amongst the early mariners from Europe, who called on the island for revictualling during their long voyages to and from their trading destinations in Asia. The turtles, who became easy prey once they had left the sea and started laying their eggs, were harvested ruthlessly and used to provide protein for scurvy-wracked sailors. The destruction of both turtles and giant land tortoises, once common to many Indian Ocean islands, was so intense in the early years of Mauritius's colonization that these reptiles virtually became extinct.

This situation has, of course, changed, but although gravid turtles could again find security on the beaches of Mauritius, its soft white sands no longer offer the stillness and solitude that these creatures of pre-history need before they are prepared to leave the relative safety of the sea to lay their eggs. Today all one can hope for is a fleeting glimpse, usually while diving, of these ancient survivors of the sea as they pass furtively by.

6 PEREYBERE
also known as PEREYBERE AQUARIUM and POISON REEF
★★

Location: The site is situated about 200m (220yds) off Péreybère Reef, opposite Péreybère beach. See map.
Access: By boat from any one of the diving centres in the North or Northwest. The boat journey takes 10-35 minutes, depending upon the location of the diving centre.
Conditions: Usually very calm with no notable currents. Visibility is around 20m (66ft), although it does sometimes deteriorate to as low as 5 or 10m (16-33ft) as a result of heavy suspension caused by dirty water reaching the dive site from nearby beaches.
Average depth: 12m (40ft)
Maximum depth: 14m (45ft)

This is a shallow dive on a flat reef. Small fish abound as it is a breeding ground. The coral reef, which shows signs of damage, has a number of nudibranchs which always make for good macro-photography. The dive is also known as Poison Reef because of the wide variety of poisonous fish that are to be found there, including: stonefish (*Synanceia verrucosa*), scorpionfish (*Scorpaenopsis gibbosa*) and the Mauritius scorpionfish (*Sebastapistes mauritiana*), firefish (*Pterois volitans*, *P. radiata* and *P. miles*), Frog fish (*Antennarius* sp.) and Leaf fish (*Taenianotus triacanthus*). Moray eels are often seen craning their necks out of crevices in the reefs and occasionally dolphins have been sighted. Notwithstanding the often dirty water that sometimes pervades the site, it is home to a large number of octopus.

7 WHALE ROCK
★★★★

Location: Whale Rock is situated just beyond the outer reef off Pointe aux Canonniers. See map.
Access: By boat from diving centres in the North and Northwest. The journey takes between 15 and 35 minutes depending on the point of departure.
Conditions: Visibility is usually good, 25-30m (82-98ft). There is normally a tidal current which at times can become fairly strong, making this a suitable drift dive. The best dives on this site are 10 days after new moon, depending on prevailing weather conditions at the time.
Average depth: 25m (82ft)
Maximum depth: 38m (125ft)

This site has a notorious history, as it is here that many ships floundered while entering or leaving the harbours of Grand Baie and Port Louis.

The bones of the ships have either rotted away or have been covered by Nature, because there are no pieces left lying about – only silent ghosts and dispassionate official entries in the annals of Mauritian nautical history remain. Whale Rock comprises a series of large black slabs of rock which are at different depths on the drop-off. Because of the varied topographical nature of the site, some diving centres divide this site into three different dives. However, since the three sites can be done in a single drift dive they will, for the purposes of this book, be treated as a single dive.

The site can be dived in two ways: by going down to 38m (125ft) and then slowly rising to 15m (49ft) using the ascent to decompress; or by starting at 15m (49ft) and then going down to 38m (125ft) with appropriate decompression at the end of the dive.

At its deepest point the dive site is characterized by large canyons and huge rocks with small caves locked in-between. Here sea fans, huge stone corals, whip coral, black coral, scorpionfish and Green moray eels (*Gymnothorax undulatus*) can be seen.

Occasionally Hammerhead sharks (*Sphyrna zygaena*) make their appearance, as do small shoals of kingfish. Swimming up to about 25m (82ft) the rock formations, as they rise, are less impressive, and the fish species change slightly to include sweetlips, parrotfish, moonfish, snappers and, occasionally, shoals of barracuda and large squid. At 20-15m (66-49ft) the variety changes again to include the smaller and prettier reef fish such as angelfish and groupers.

8 GRAVEYARD
★★

Location: The dive is situated approximately 1km (just over half a mile) from Grand Baie, to the left of the pass through the barrier reef. See map.
Access: By boat from any one of the diving centres operating in the North and Northwest.
Conditions: The sea conditions are normally very calm with only an occasional gentle tidal current. Visibility is good, 20-30m (66-98ft) and in ideal conditions it often exceeds 60m (197ft).
Average depth: 15m (49ft)
Maximum depth: 20m (66ft)

The site is made up of a rocky reef encrusted with coral, much of which is dead – hence the name Graveyard. The fauna and flora is poor, but the site has some interest because of the wide variety of shells one can find (again many of which are dead). Typical shells to be seen include cowries (*Cypraea* sp.), spider conchs (*Lambis* sp.) and various cone species including the poisonous *Conus geographicus* and *C. textalis*. Always keep in mind that they should not be removed.

Turret corals, when closed, are tall and turret-like, but when open, they resemble a sea of flowers.

9 FLAT ISLAND

★★★★

Location: Flat Island lies north of Coin de Mire. See map.
Access: By boat from diving centres situated in the North and Northwest. The journey takes between 20 and 45 minutes depending on the point of departure and on the type of boat used.
Conditions: Only dived during summer months when the sea is calmer. The best diving is during neap tide.
Average depth: 20m (66ft)
Maximum depth: 24m (79ft)

Flat Island is made up of three different elements. The first is the island itself, the second is a very small island called Gabriel Island and the third is a rock that protrudes from the sea called Pigeon House Rock. At Gabriel Island there is a sheltered, shallow cove that is full of life and makes a very interesting place to snorkel.

Scuba diving takes place around Pigeon House Rock where the main attraction is the proliferation of sharks that gather there, particularly during the period November to April.

Diving conditions are not ideal as there is invariably a heavy surge and the sea can be rough. Because of these conditions and the dangers that they present to divers, diving at Flat Island has to be specially arranged and not all the diving centres in the area are prepared to take divers who are not known to them to the site.

Please note that only highly experienced divers are considered for diving at this particular site, and then only if conditions are right. When and if all these factors come together, there is a rich reward for those who manage to make it.

10 BAIN BOEUF

★★★★

Location: This site is situated outside the reef, 1.5km (1 mile) from the coast, between Cap Malheureux and Péreybère. See map.
Access: By boat and the site is served by a number of diving centres operating in the region.
Conditions: The dive site is subject to a gentle current of up to two knots, therefore a drift dive would be the usual option to take. Visibility is usually good with the average distance exceeding 20m (66ft).
Average depth: 20m (66ft)
Maximum depth: 27m (89ft)

The dive starts at 27m (89ft) and slowly ascends up to 14m (46ft). The main features of this dive are the hard and soft corals, which are in good condition in the deeper areas.

There are usually large shoals of snappers, while a variety of triggerfish are seen from time to time.

11 ANEMONE
also known as ANEMONE TILLA

★★★

Location: The dive site is situated close to Péreybère and Pointe d'Azur (see No. 4. Pointe Vacoas, and No. 6. Péreybère) off Pointe Taylor. See map.
Access: Access is by boat from any one of the diving centres operating in the North or Northwest subregions. The journey takes between 10 and 30 minutes depending on the point of departure.
Conditions: Conditions are normally favourable throughout the year. Visibility is usually very good, seldom dropping below 25m (82ft) and often exceeding 50m (164ft).
Average depth: 19m (62ft)
Maximum depth: 27m (89ft)

The dive site is situated on a large reef, which accommodates two other dive sites (*see* No. 4. Pointe Vacoas, page 88, and No. 6. Péreybère, page 92). This dive site is covered in sea anemones that play host to a great number of anemonefish that hover about, quickly hiding in the waving tentacles of their hosts whenever danger comes too close for comfort.

There is also a wide variety of tropical fish, many of which are immature, including damselfish, angelfish, squirrelfish and soldierfish. Occasionally parrotfish come bustling through this area. Both pufferfish (*Arothron hispidus*) and balloonfish (*Diodon hystrix*) are permanent residents on the reef.

12 THE *SILVER STAR*

★★★★

Location: The *Silver Star* lies some 2km (1.25 mile) offshore at a depth of 38m (125ft), just through the pass at Grand Baie directly opposite the Royal Palm Hotel. See map.
Access: By boat from any one of the dive centres operating in the North or Northwest subregions.
Conditions: Conditions are normally very good, with visibility between 20 and 25m (66-82ft) and on occasion reaching up to 50m (164ft). At the time of the new moon the site may be washed by a gentle tidal current. The conditions are normally very good for wreck-diving.
Average depth: The ship's crow's nest is at approximately 22m (72ft) and the bottom of the ship lies at 39m (128ft).
Maximum depth: 39m (128ft)

The *Silver Star* was sunk to create an artificial reef in December 1992. It is an interesting dive because the ship landed upright with its bow resting on a small reef and the remainder of its bulk sitting on the sea's sandy floor.

An interesting feature of the wreck is that it was only stripped of those things that could cause pollution or that could become a problem through corrosion: the engine was drained of its oil, its bunkers were emptied and some of its wiring and instruments removed. The ship's dignity has thus been maintained – even the vessel's propeller is still intact and its previous owners are to be saluted for their lack of parsimony. Life has begun to grow on the ship's rusting plates: large pink soft corals are steadily gathering in various places. A particularly interesting display of soft corals has already begun to take shape on the mast above the crow's nest and this should not be missed. Hard corals are beginning to form in a number of places on the ship and many species of interesting marine flora are evident.

If seeing a ship, lying still virtually intact in gloomy water at the bottom of the sea excites you, and studying the development of a variety of marine growth interests you, then this dive is a must.

SEA FANS AND SEA PENS

Gorgonians (sea fans) form colonies which branch out from a central base and leave the impression of a small tree, or a fan. They are made of gorgonin – a horn-like protein that is covered with small polyps. A Pennatulacea (sea pen) is much softer, with a fleshy body. It is covered with polyps and has a soft, unbranched stalk (peduncle) that anchors the colony to a rock or to the sea floor.

DIVING COSTS

The cost per dive ranges between Rs500 and Rs650, depending on the amount of equipment hired by the diver. It is also possible to negotiate cheaper rates on a package basis. The cost of training ranges from Rs750 for a basic Introduction to Diving to around Rs7000 for a CMAS One-Star diving course.

DIVING CENTRES

Diving centres belonging to the Mauritian Scuba Diving Association (MSDA) are as follows:

• **Paradise Diving Centre**, Grand Baie. Tel 263-7220 Fax: 263-8534

Paradise Diving is affiliated to CMAS and NAUI and operates from:

• Grand Baie, town centre
• Hibiscus, Village Vacances, Péreybère
• PLM Azur Hotel, Trou aux Biches

The company has the following equipment which is moved between each centre according to demand:
Boats: one 40ft Catamaran yacht, a 27ft fibreglass specialized dive boat and a 25ft wooden pirogue.
Tanks: A total of 30 10- and 12-litre aluminium tanks.
A full range of wetsuits to fit all sizes plus masks and fins to equip 20 divers.
20 Dacor regulators and 20 Sea Quest bouyancy compensators.
Training is centralized at Grand Baie and a full range of diving courses is offered – from an Introduction to Diving to Divemaster and Assistant Instructor. (Advance warning is required in order to arrange for an overseas examiner.)
A staff of four divemasters and nine support people are employed.

• **Diving World**, Le Mauricia Hotel. Tel: 263-7800 Fax: 263-7888

Diving World has a full range of Scubapro equipment and is able to completely kit out 12 divers. All tanks are steel and have a carrying capacity of 9, 12 or 15 litres. The centre offers training, from an Introduction to Diving to CMAS One-Star certification.

• **Islandive Ltd.**, Veranda Bungalow Village. Tel: 263-8015 Fax: 263-7369

Islandive is a registered member of the MSDA and has two diving centres: one at Veranda Bungalow Village, between Le Mauricia Hotel and Grand Baie Yacht Club, in Grand Baie, and the other at Grand Gaube Hotel to the east of Anse La Raie. Through this expansion, Islandive is able to offer its services to a broad range of clientele. The company has a full range of equipment for hire and has sufficient to completely kit out 30 divers. Islandive operates three custom-built dive boats, all of which are equipped with medical and oxygen supplies. Islandive is a PADI/NAUI/CMAS dive school and offers courses from an Introduction to Diving to advanced levels within each of these associations.

• **Merville Diving Centre**, Le Merville Hotel, Grand Baie. Tel: 263-8621 Fax: 263-8146

Merville Diving is a registered member of MSDA and is CMAS-affiliated. It offers training from an introductory course to diving to Three-Star certification. All equipment is Scubapro and the centre has sets to fully equip 12 divers. All tanks are 12-litre steel.
The centre operates a 25ft wooden boat which is powered by two 25HP motors.

• **Dolphin Diving Centre**, Royal Road, Grand Baie. Tel: 263-7273

Dolphin Diving operates from premises in Péreybère, is CMAS- and DIWA-affiliated and provides training from an introductory course to Two-Star certification. The centre has sufficient Scubapro and Spirotechnique equipment to fully kit out 15 divers, as well as a choice between 10-, 12- or 15-litre capacity bottles.

• **The Cap Divers Ltd.**, Le Paradise Hotel, Anse La Raie. Tel: 262-7983 Fax: 262-7736

The centre has immediate access to the jetty to which the dive boat is tethered – a great convenience for divers. Cap

Divers has a full range of Scubapro and Poseidon equipment for 15 divers, and operates the following three boats:
1. A large and comfortable 27x10ft mono-hull glassfibre boat powered by a 135HP and a 120HP Johnson motor;
2. A mono-hull 21x9ft glassfibre boat with twin 50HP Johnson motors; and
3. A mono-hull 18x6ft glassfibre boat which is based at Cap Divers' premises in Grand Baie. This boat is used when the weather at Anse La Raie is variable, and for night diving.

Cap Divers also operates a dive centre at Belle Mare Plage Hotel on the east coast which it coordinates with the services it provides at Paradise Cove.

• **Sindbad Ltd.**, Kux Village, Cap Malheureux. Tel: 262-8836 Fax: 262-7407

The centre is affiliated to CMAS and DIWA and has a full range of equipment for 15 divers. It presently operates a 26ft inboard diesel-powered diving boat.
Sindbad offers comprehensive training – from beginner courses right through to Diving Instructor (for which advance notice is required). Underwater photography, including video dubbing and cutting services, are also offered.

SPORT AND RECREATIONAL ACTIVITIES

Watersports
Water-skiing, windsurfing, yachting, riding in a *pedalo*, parasailing and trips in a fibreglass-bottomed boat are offered by most hotels in the Grand Baie area.

Deep-sea fishing
Mauritius offers spectacular deep-sea fishing opportunities, particularly between October and March. Fishing trips can be arranged through the reception for guests at beach hotels and nonresidents can make arrangements directly with:

Sportfisher, Royal Road, Grand Baie. Tel: 263-8358

Le Corsaire Club de Pêche du Nord, Royal Road, Trou aux Biches. Tel: 261-6264 Fax: 261-6611

The luxurious Cotton Bay Hotel, on the eastern tip of Rodrigues.

A tiny island surrounded by the Indian Ocean, Rodrigues is only 18km (11 miles) long and 8km (5 miles) wide. It lies some 560km (348 miles) east of Mauritius. Situated virtually on the same line of latitude as Mauritius, Rodrigues has a similar climate and vegetation to the larger island. Both islands are volcanic in origin, so their physical features are likewise very similar.

With the exception of a few narrow passes the island is virtually encircled by coral reefs which lie, in some places, as much as five nautical miles offshore. Consequently, diving on the island is divided into two broad categories: within the confines of the perimeter coral reefs (i.e. in the surrounding lagoons), and beyond the reef in the deep sea. Diving in the lagoon is typically within deep ravines that have been gouged out of the reef floor by aeons of tidal action. Within these ravines currents are invariably strong, and visibility seldom exceeds 15m (49ft), making these dive sites unsuitable for beginners. These ravines are, however, important fish-feeding grounds, so divers are rewarded with some spectacular sightings of a variety of tropical fish.

In addition the ravine walls are lined with coral while many of the rock formations are weather-worn into strange and almost grotesque contortions which are always intriguing and constantly challenging.

In the words of author T.V. Bulpin (*Islands in a Forgotten Sea*), diving outside the lagoon opens '... jewellery boxes of the sea (where) there lives a fantastic variety of strange and colourful creatures. In fact, there can be few places on earth inhabited more densely than the dreamlike jungles of these coral reefs.'

These jewellery boxes still contain most of their treasures because Rodrigues is commercially undeveloped and essentially 'off the beaten track'.

As a result there has been little exploitation and pressure to dull the lustre of this island's sparkling jewels.

There is only one dive centre on the island, the La Licorne Dive Centre, which is situated at Rodrigues' only luxury beach resort, the Cotton Bay Hotel, on the east coast. The centre has a full range of equipment and can kit out eight divers completely. It operates its own boat and has access to a second boat should the need arise. La Licorne Dive Centre is a registered member of the Mauritius Scuba Diving Association (MSDA).

As Rodrigues does not have its own recompression chamber, it is very cautious in its diving practice. No dives deeper than 30m (98ft), or requiring decompression, are ever undertaken and on all dives deeper than 12m (39ft), a precautionary decompression stop is compulsory.

A comprehensive medical kit, including oxygen, is always carried on the boat. Two 20-litre cylinders of oxygen are available at the dive centre.

A total of 17 dive sites have been identified to date and regular use is made of at least 14 of them.

For further information on diving in Rodrigues contact should be established with: La Licorne Dive Centre, Cotton Bay Hotel. Tel: 831-2179 Fax: 831-1959

A local Rodriguan fisherman.

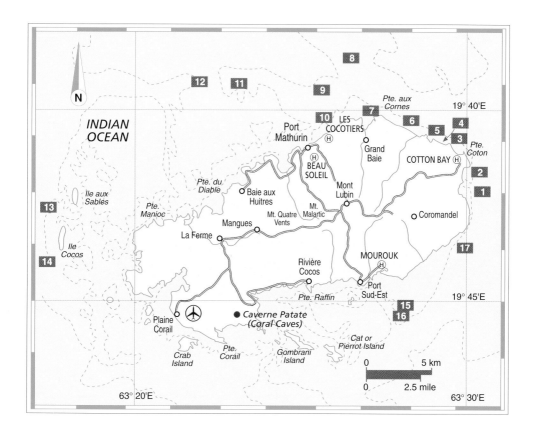

THE EAST

This subregion stretches from Grand Gaube in the north to Mahébourg in the south. However, because of prevailing winds and rough seas, organized diving only takes place at four places along this coastline, namely at Pointe de Flacq (from the St Géran and the Belle Mare hotels), Palmar (from Hotel Ambre), Belle Mare (from Belle Mare Plage Hotel), and Trou d'Eau Douce (from Le Touessrok Hotel). Between Grand Gaube and Pointe de Flacq in the east there are very few tourist facilities and diving in this area is only done by locals who have their own equipment. Between Trou d'Eau Douce and Mahébourg in the south, the reef is broken and the sea rough, so no organized diving is done here.

Flacq comes from the Dutch word *vlakte* which means plains – an apt description of the low-lying area that is only broken by an occasional hill or undulation. It is a very pleasant and prosperous corner of Mauritius, much wetter than in the north and in earlier times the area was covered in dense forests of large ebony trees. These were exploited by the Dutch in the 17th century. Today it is a rich sugar-plantation area and the island's largest sugar estate is located here. A number of well-preserved old lime kilns can be seen along this part of the coast. Just north of Belle Mare the remains of an old sugar factory with its three large chimneys, still intact, can be seen. The first steam-powered mill was erected here by Adrien d'Epinay in 1822. Near Belle Mare there is a marble cenotaph erected in memory of the 159 passengers and crew who died following the crash of the Helderberg – a Boeing 747 aircraft belonging to South African Airways, in November 1987.

DIVING CONDITIONS
Most of the diving centres operating in this region are based in or around passes through the coral barrier reefs which are specific to each dive centre. Drift dives are invariably done, subject to tidal currents. Water temperatures are standard throughout the subregion and average from 18–22°C (64–72°F) in winter, and from 24–26°C (75–79°F) in summer.

Left: *A secluded beach villa on the East Coast depicts the calm and tranquil atmosphere that pervades Mauritius's coastline.* Above: *Sea goldies, usually gregarious, are common reef-dwellers and feed on plankton.*

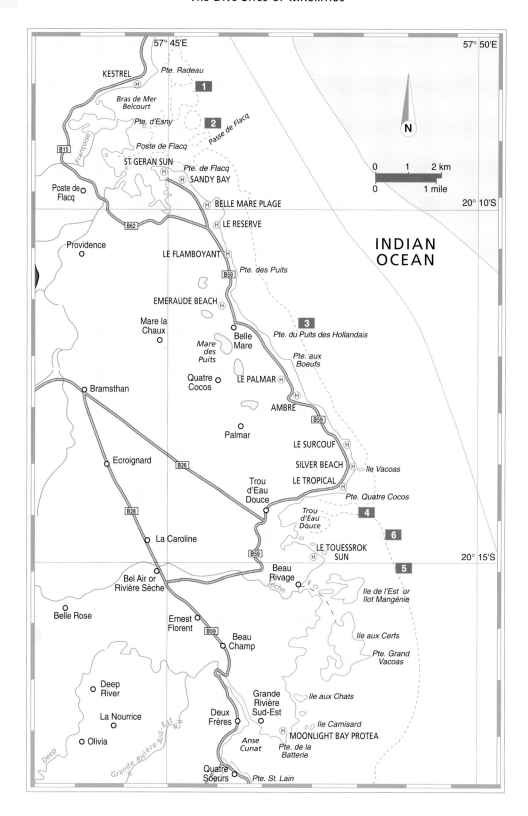

57° 45'E

57° 50'E

KESTREL Ⓗ

Pte. Radeau

1

Bras de Mer
Belcourt

Pte. d'Esny

2

Passe de Flacq

Poste de Flacq

B15

Françoise

ST GERAN SUN

Pte. de Flacq

Ⓗ SANDY BAY

Poste de Ⓞ
Flacq

Ⓗ BELLE MARE PLAGE

B62

20° 10'S

Ⓗ LE RESERVE

Providence
Ⓞ

INDIAN
OCEAN

LE FLAMBOYANT Ⓗ

B59

Pte. des Puits

EMERAUDE BEACH Ⓗ

Mare la
Chaux
Ⓞ

Belle
Mare

3

Mare
des
Puits

Pte. du Puits des Hollandais

Pte. aux
Boeufs

Quatre Ⓞ
Cocos

LE PALMAR Ⓗ

Bramsthan Ⓞ

AMBRE

Ⓗ

B59

Palmar
Ⓞ

LE SURCOUF Ⓗ

Ecroignard
Ⓞ

B26

SILVER BEACH

Ile Vacaos

LE TROPICAL Ⓗ

B28

Trou
d'Eau
Douce

Pte. Quatre Cocos

La Caroline Ⓞ

Trou
d'Eau
Douce

4

6

B59

LE TOUESSROK
SUN Ⓗ

20° 15'S

Bel Air or
Rivière Sèche Ⓞ

Beau
Rivage

5

Sèche

Belle Rose
Ⓞ

Ernest Ⓞ
Florent

B59

Beau
Champ
Ⓞ

Ile de l'Est or
Ilot Mangénie

Ile aux Cerfs

Pte. Grand
Vacaos

Deep
River
Ⓞ

Grande
Rivière
Sud-Est

Ile aux Chats

La Nourrice
Ⓞ

Deux
Frères
Ⓞ

Ile Camisard

Ⓞ Olivia

Grande Rivière sud-Est

Deep

Anse
Cunat

Pte. de la
Batterie

Ⓗ MOONLIGHT BAY PROTEA

Quatre
Soeurs Ⓞ

Pte. St. Lain

N

0   1   2 km

0   1 mile

The popular dive sites in the East sub-region are as follows:

1 LOBSTER CANYON

★ ★ ★

Location: The site lies approximately 500m (547yds) beyond the reef and about 1.6km (1 mile) from the beach, northeast of the St Géran hotel. See map.
Access: From all diving centres operating in the area by boat through the Passe Canon. The journey takes about 15 minutes from the dive centre at St Géran.
Conditions: During the winter season, between June and August, the southeast trade winds blow strongly and good diving conditions are infrequent during this period. The best diving is done from September to May when the prevailing winds usually die down, except during cyclonic weather. The site is subject to a 3-4 knot current during high spring tides when it is not possible to dive. However, most of the time the current is only slight. Visibility is between 10 and 20m (33-66ft), due to fairly high levels of plankton in the water. In ideal conditions visibility averages between 25 and 35m (82-115ft).
Average depth: 20m (66ft)
Maximum depth: 25m (82ft)

The dive proceeds along a gully, through a short cave full of crayfish (lobsters), then along a wall and into a canyon. At times small White-tip sharks (*Triaenodon obesus*) are seen in the canyon. Shoals of Blueline snappers (*Lutjanus caeruleolineatus*) are common and both Giant and Bluefin kingfish (*Caranx ignobilis* and *C. melampygus*) pause for a moment before swimming on: they are worth watching. Eagle-rays are frequent visitors to the dive site.

2 THE PASS

★ ★ ★

Location: This dive begins in the pass through the barrier reef, east of the St Géran hotel, and continues for some 2km (1.25 miles) in an easterly direction. See map.
Access: By boat (approximately 5 minutes from the dive centre at the St Géran hotel).
Conditions: Drift diving using the outflowing current through the pass. The dive is weather-dependent and it is not suitable for all conditions.
Average depth: 16-18m (52-59ft)
Maximum depth: 25m (82ft)

This is a drift dive which begins at 8m (26ft) at the mouth of the pass and proceeds through the pass descending to 17m (56ft) for much of the dive and culminating some 2km (1.25 miles) east of the barrier reef at 25m (82ft). En route the diver floats through a cross section of daily life in a busy sea. There are occasional clouds of small tropical fish busily going about the business of eating their daily food; various species of parrotfish – always a riot of colour and design – come past, occasionally pecking at a piece of coral and then quickly moving on. Sometimes turtles come gliding into view; they may circle the diver, banking steeply as they try to get a better view of the awkward, bubbling strangers passing through, and then with a few strokes of their flippers they disappear into the gloom. Sharks are seen frequently, their streamlined design and effortless grace never failing to impress. There is always something to look at. The essence of the dive is surprise, surprise!

FISH AND SEX CHANGE

Many reef fish change their sex during their life span, a phenomenon known as reversal hermaphroditism. Some fish are protandrous, that is, they begin life as males and then change to females at a later stage. Or they may be protogynous, which means that they start life as females and then switch sex to become males. Other fish are monandrous, in other words, they are all one sex when they are born, and collectively change to the other.

The process of changing sex is usually socially controlled. With protogynous hermaphrodites, such as wrasses and parrotfishes, the presence of terminal males (i.e. fully matured) inhibits females from changing their sex; equally with fish that have a haremic social system, in other words, there is one dominant male over a group of females (for example angelfish). The presence of the dominant male prevents the females from changing their sex. Should anything happen to that male, for example, should he be taken by a predator, the most aggressive female will change her sex and become the dominant male!

In protandrous hermaphrodites, such as the anemonefishes, the reverse situation applies. In a typical large anemone there is usually a single pair of reproductively active anemonefish and one or more immature individuals. The largest and most dominant fish is female and should she be removed, the male will change his sex and become female, while the largest juvenile will become the new male of the pair.

The reason for sex change is Nature's clever way of ensuring that fish that are normally territorial and confined to a defined space can continue to procreate should an imbalance occur in the ratio of the sexes. Should this happen, a quick sex change ensures that egg production and fertilization continue and so does the species.

3 LA PASSE DE BELLE MARE

★★★ to ★★★★

Location: The site comprises an area that is approximately 2km long and 1.5km wide (1.25; 1 miles), and is located on the seaward side of the pass through the barrier reef near the Belle Mare Plage Hotel. It comprises five separate but interdependent dive sites which can be dived individually or as part of an integrated package. See map.

Access: By boat from the St Géran, Belle Mare Plage and Ambre hotels. The trip takes between 10 and 30 minutes depending on point of departure.

Conditions: Diving in the La Passe area is subject to tidal flow and therefore to currents of variable strengths, depending on the phases of the moon and the time of day. Dives are usually drift dives. Visibility is variable, ranging mostly between 15 and 25m (49-82ft), but occasionally going up to as much as 35m (115ft), and down to as little as 10m (33ft), when plankton levels increase. Currents vary quite considerably between the different constituent dives within the composite area.

Average depth: 20m (66ft)
Maximum depth: 33m (108ft)

The separate components culminating to form the La Passe de Belle Mare site can be dived singly or they can be combined in a number of different ways to make up a variety of different dives. The major characteristics of each of the components making up the La Passe dive area are the following:

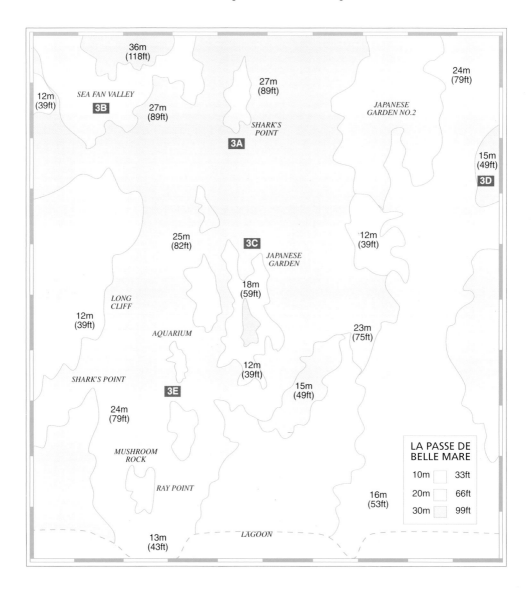

36m
(118ft)

27m
(89ft)

24m
(79ft)

12m
(39ft)

SEA FAN VALLEY

3B

27m
(89ft)

JAPANESE
GARDEN NO.2

SHARK'S
POINT

3A

15m
(49ft)

3D

25m
(82ft)

3C

JAPANESE
GARDEN

12m
(39ft)

18m
(59ft)

LONG
CLIFF

12m
(39ft)

AQUARIUM

23m
(75ft)

12m
(39ft)

SHARK'S POINT

3E

15m
(49ft)

24m
(79ft)

MUSHROOM
ROCK

RAY POINT

16m
(53ft)

LA PASSE DE
BELLE MARE

10m		33ft
20m		66ft
30m		99ft

13m
(43ft)

LAGOON

A. Shark Point: The outstanding feature of this dive site is the range and number of pelagic fish species that can be seen on most dives.

Shoals of barracuda are common: seldom will a diver see less than 10 Black-tip reef sharks (*Carcharhinus melanopterus*) on a single dive in summer; eagle-rays frequently make a graceful appearance; kingfish are constant companions to divers, while typical tropical reef fish are always there to hold your attention when there is a pause in the performance of the other, bigger fish.

On its own this dive site warrants a maximum three-star rating.

B. Sea Fan Valley: This site is characterized by a variety of sea fans and pens and at 30m (98ft) there is an area of approximately 50m^2 (500ft^2) in which a garden of gorgonians of all different shapes and sizes grow. A variety of tropical fish adds colour and interest to the dive site. This is a relaxing and colourful dive that requires maximum use of time. For this reason divemasters are reluctant to take inexperienced divers, because most of the dive is deep, and also because inexperienced divers tend to use up their air too quickly, thus shortening the dive time for the more experienced divers in the party.

As an individual dive this site also warrants at least a three-star rating.

C. Japanese Garden: This site comprises an area where there is a mass of low coral, varying interestingly in shape and colour. These provide a backdrop for the tropical fish that gather there. Because of the general lack of current and the shallowness of the dive area, the dive is usually used as a pass-out site for beginners.

The Japanese Garden warrants a two-star rating.

D. Castle: This site is made up of a combination of hard and soft corals and has a variety of tropical fish.

The dive is an attractive site which is used especially by photographers and for night diving, and as such warrants a four-star rating.

E. Aquarium: This dive takes place on a series of rocky outcrops that are situated in the main channel of the pass. The outstanding feature of this site is the variety of fish that can be seen here.

The dive deserves a three-star rating.

Le Passe de Belle Mare offers a selection of dive sites that can be incorporated in a single dive (depending on current and weather conditions at the time of the dive), and that can be very exciting and are highly recommended.

A notable feature of the area is the variety of marine activity that takes place, and the interplay between major actors in the daily drama of underwater life. For example, between December and March, during ovulation, eagle-rays gather in the *Japanese Garden* area and actually attack sharks. Their plan of attack and its execution is a study in military strategic planning and

The 'Aquarium' is an underwater paradise, teeming with a variety of exquisite fish.

co-ordination: the rays gather into a large group of some 20 to 30 members and then, as if receiving a silent command, five or six of them hive off to seek out and provoke a shark. The shark responds quickly and makes ready for the kill, following the rays who head them to the rest of the group. The moment the shark is in sight of the awaiting rays they swoop down and bombard it, forcing the shark down onto the reef's floor.

This incredible spectacle often results in the death of the shark, but on more occasions than not, it manages to get away, often just badly bruised.

At *Shark Point* it is possible to see sharks passing by as they comb the sea in search of prey. While sightings cannot be guaranteed on every dive, it is not often that

Fish sequins present a brilliant display of flashing light underwater.

divers are disappointed. Dolphins too make regular appearances and treat divers to a charming and elegant display of their grace and agility.

They have also been seen by divers (on very rare and privileged occasions) to display great aggression towards sharks. A school of dolphins has been observed in the act of 'dive-bombing' sharks – swooping down at full speed on the unsuspecting animals and crashing into them beak-first. Few sharks manage to survive this sort of pounding by dolphins.

It is even possible to observe an entire hunting cycle being played out before your eyes: a large shoal of barracuda will swim by, unaware of the streamlined tuna in the deep water. From out of the blue, the tuna suddenly attack. As they grab a fish they pivot vertically on their tails in order to facilitate the swallowing process. Then, often, in a flash, the tuna is attacked by a shark, and there is a moment of frenzied action.

Seconds later all is calm again, and the steady rhythm of the sea beats on.

Another unusual event witnessed by some very fortunate divers is a marine 'dogfight': a shark lines up a shoal of kingfish and prepares to attack, the fish accelerate and as the shark moves in for the kill the kingfish, in perfect unison, do a quick vertical loop and, in single file, tuck into the slipstream immediately behind the shark – keeping out of its line of vision. As the shark moves about in search of its evasive prey, the kingfish follow it, keeping precisely within its watery tracks. Eventually the shark gives up, and when the fish sense this they quickly move off in another direction.

Swimming with Spotted eagle-rays (*Aetobatus narinari*) is a great attraction at Ray Point (*see* map page 100). When conditions are right, rays sometimes swim against the outgoing tide at this point and then, as one, they do a half-roll and swoop back to Long Cliff. As they do this the waiting divers, gathered in the lee of a rock in anticipation, join the rays and swim together with these graceful hovercrafts of the sea. The rays seem to revel in the divers' bubbles and great fun is had by all. On reaching Long Cliff, the rays return for a repeat performance, but the divers cannot follow their momentary playmates as the current is too strong for them to swim against.

In the *Japanese Garden* area a particular Yellow-fin tuna has been seen to perform the inexplicable act of 'standing' on its tail, body vibrating as it moves its tail from side to side in order to hold its position, while a remora cleans its teeth!

4 LE TOUESSROK PASS

★★

Location: Le Touessrok Pass is less than 10 minutes by boat from the diving centre, and is situated in the pass through the barrier reef in front of Le Touessrok Hotel.
Access: By boat from the diving centre.
Conditions: The dive site is subject to tidal currents which vary according to the time of day and the time of month. Visibility is between 20 and 25m (66-82ft).
Average depth: 22m (72ft)
Maximum depth: 26m (85ft)

This is usually a drift dive and divers are treated to an interesting variety of fish, including shoals of Somber sweetlips (*Plectorhinchus schotaf*), parrotfish, groupers – of which the dominant species is the Honeycomb grouper (*Epinephelus merra*) – Blotcheye soldierfish (*Myripristis murdjan*), squirrelfish, Mauritius hogfish (*Bodianus macrourus*), various species of goatfish and occasionally tuna and stingrays. The base of the pass is made up of a sandy floor interspersed with large boulders.

5 THE WALL

★★

Location: The site is situated 1km (a little over half a mile) south of the pass through the reef, just off the outer edge.
Access: By boat from the diving centre at Le Touessrok Hotel. The journey takes approximately 25 minutes.
Conditions: The site is weather-dependent and often cannot be dived because of strong winds and rough seas. When conditions are settled, visibility averages between 20 and 25m (66-82ft) and can even exceed 35m (115ft).
Average depth: 23m (75ft)
Maximum depth: 25m (82ft)

The dive site consists of a long, high reef surrounded by sand. The actual length of the reef is approximately 400m (437yds) and it can be dived as two dives – first on the one side and then on the other.

A wide variety of marine life can be seen on this reef, including both tropical reef and pelagic fish. Those fish that are frequently seen include parrotfish, a variety of triggerfish – notable amongst these is the Clown trigger-fish *(Balistoides conspicillum)* – surgeonfish, groupers, Blacktongue unicorn fish *(Naso hexacanthus)*, moray eels, angelfish, shoals of fusiliers and occasionally barracuda and tuna.

This is an interesting dive, but unfortunately the unreliability of the weather and the adverse effect this has on the dive makes it suitable only if you are on the spot.

6 DRIFT DIVE

★★★

Location: This site is situated between Le Touessrok Pass and The Wall *(see No.s 4. and 5., page 105).*
Access: By boat from Le Touessrok Hotel.
Conditions: As with The Wall, this site is also weather-dependent but, as it is located nearer to the reef the site is a little more protected and therefore less vulnerable to the vagaries of weather.
Average depth: 17m (56ft)
Maximum depth: 23m (75ft)

CLEANER SHRIMPS

A cleaner shrimp *(Stenopus hispidus)* is an interesting little creature. It is strikingly coloured, with red and white bands tinged with blue on its body and on its long legs which end in pincers. It has long white antennae that move gently about, constantly sensing for the direction of possible danger.

These shrimps are normally located in crevices or at the entrances of small caves, and if the diver is very patient and still, he can watch an extraordinary and interesting act of Nature as fish come to the shrimps to have parasites and bacterial growth removed. You can sometimes watch a 'queue' form as fish await their turn to be cleaned.

This dive takes place on a relatively flat, coral-encrusted reef which is in good condition. The reef supports a wide variety of changing tropical reef fish life, which makes each dive on the site a different experience.

Honeycomb groupers are commonly found in Indian Ocean coral reefs.

DIVING COSTS

The cost of a dive ranges from Rs450 (for a lagoon dive) to Rs600, and the hire of equipment is usually included in this amount, irrespective of whether the diver brings his own gear or not.

DIVING CENTRES

Organized diving only takes place at four places along this section of the Mauritian coastline, namely at:

• Poste de Flacq, where East Coast Diving Ltd. operates from the St Géran Hotel.
• Belle Mare, where The Cap Divers Ltd. operates from the Belle Mare Plage Hotel.
• Palmar, where Explorer Diving Centre operates from the Hotel Ambre.
• Trou d'Eau Douce, where Pierre Sport Diving Ltd. operates from the Le Touessrok Hotel.

All diving centres operating in this subregion offer training courses – from introductory up to Divemaster courses, although the usual is up to the CMAS One-Star certification.

Virtually all the dive sites used by these diving centres are based in or around passes through the coral barrier reefs, and are, in almost all cases, specific to each dive centre.

Dives are invariably drift dives and are subject to tidal currents which vary according to the phases of the moon. The diving centres belonging to the Mauritius Scuba Diving Association (MSDA) operating in this subregion are as follows:

• **East Coast Diving Ltd.**,
St. Géran Hotel, Poste de Flacq.
Tel: 416-1825 Fax: 415-1983

Due to the variability of prevailing weather conditions along the east coast, the diving centre also has access to facilities at Grand Baie and can take divers there when conditions in this region are unpleasant or difficult.

The centre has sufficient equipment to fully kit out 10 divers. All equipment is Spirotechnique and includes 10-, 12-

and 15-litre bottles. East Coast Diving operates a 30x8ft wooden boat that is powered by twin 25HP Suzuki motors.

Training is offered from basics up to a CMAS One-Star certificate.

• **The Cap Divers Ltd.**,
Belle Mare Plage Hotel, Poste de Flacq.
Tel: 413-2518 Fax: 413-2993

At present Cap Divers is concentrating on offering training, from an introductory course to Three-Star certification. Both diving and training, as well as the hire of equipment at the Belle Mare Plage Hotel, are co-ordinated with Cap Divers' operation at Anse La Raie.

However, the two operations will be separated shortly and a fully-fledged, semi-independent branch will be established at Belle Mare Plage Hotel in 1995.

• **Explorer Diving Centre**,
Hotel Ambre, Palmar, Belle Mare.
Tel: 415-1544 Fax:415-1594

Explorer offers services and facilities primarily to guests of the hotel, but also to visitors in the region. The centre has a full range of Scubapro and Beuchat equipment and can cater for a maximum of 20 divers at a time. Explorer supplies both steel and aluminium cylinders which range in capacity from 8-litre bottles for pool training to 12- and 15-litre bottles for diving. All equipment hire costs are included in the cost of the dive, irrespective of whether the diver brings his own gear or not.

The centre has two boats and operates two dives a day, at 09:30 and 14:00, but during the season four dives are offered. All dives take place in 'La Passe De Belle Mare' which is about 500m (547yds) from the Ambre Hotel. For those interested in wreck diving, the centre arranges special trips to the *Silver Star* and the *Stella Maru* in the North and Northwest subregions. Night dives can be arranged on request.

• **Pierre Sport Diving**,
Le Touessrok Hotel, Trou d'Eau Douce.
Tel: 419-2451 Fax: 419-2025

This centre provides a personalized service to hotel guests. Pierre Sport uses three local dive sites, but has arrange-

ments with most diving centres around the island, and guests can be transported to the centre of their choice.

The cost of transport is divided equally among participating divers. The centre has a boat stationed permanently at Grand Baie and is able to offer guests a full range of dives in the North.

Pierre Sport can equip 15 divers with a full range of gear, including a choice of either 10- or 15-litre steel tanks. All equipment is Spirotechnique. The centre operates a 4m (13ft) wooden mono-hull boat which is powered by twin 25HP motors. The staff of three offer training from a basic introductory course to a CMAS One-Star certificate.

SPORT AND RECREATIONAL ACTIVITIES

Watersports
Water-skiing, windsurfing, yachting, riding in a *pedalo*, parasailing and trips in a fibreglass-bottomed boat are offered by most hotels. All resort hotels have swimming pools around which residents can laze if they prefer to avoid the beach.

Hiking
• *Domaine du Chasseur and the Bambous mountains*

Domaine du Chasseur is a private estate on which deer hunting takes place during the season. Off season it is possible to follow the hunting trails across the trackless hills of the Bambous mountains which fall within the estate. There are lovely views through forest patches and down to the sea.

Social games
Most beach hotels have tennis, squash and volleyball courts. St Géran has a nine-hole golf course set in a spectacular palm grove.

EATING OUT

All beach hotels operating in this subregion structure their tariffs on a dinner, bed and breakfast basis, and therefore almost all guests eat at their hotel's restaurants. Due to the relatively isolated nature of the east coast there are few good restaurants (outside of the hotels) that are worth mentioning.

THE SOUTH

The South is perceived by many as the 'Wild Coast' – the Costa Brava of Mauritius. This is the part of the island that is met first by the onshore southeast trade winds, and so diving beyond the barrier reef is often restricted as the seas are too rough. But the South also has Blue Bay and Grand Port Bay (where the first mariners to Mauritius anchored their ships and where the English and French slogged it out in deadly battle in 1810). These are large lagoons with prolific coral colonies which are protected from the ravages of the open seas by the barrier reef and which provide the only lagoon scuba diving in Mauritius. At Blue Bay (where the luxurious Shandrani Hotel is situated on golden shores) it is possible to dive throughout the year, irrespective of wind and weather conditions, because it is so well protected. Diving beyond the reef is done along the drop-off. Wave action and the various forces of Nature have created deep caves and long canyons, tunnels and crevices in the drop-off which provide many interesting dive sites. Between Blue Bay in the north of this subregion and Le Morne in the southwest there are no diving centres, so no organized diving takes place there at all. There are also relatively few beaches where it is safe to swim.

DIVING CONDITIONS

Organized diving in the South is, at present, concentrated in the area between Mahébourg and Blue Bay. However, new dive sites are constantly being discovered as more areas are explored and mapped. Diving here in the open sea is more problematic because of prevailing weather conditions, as has already been mentioned. Normally weather conditions are more favourable in summer than in winter (except, of course, during cyclonic periods when diving is not possible anywhere on the island). Water temperatures vary between the lagoon and the open sea, and in relation to winter and summer conditions. In the lagoon, temperatures range from 26–30°C (79–86°F) in summer to 22–25°C (72–77°F) in winter; in the open sea from 24–26°C (75–79°F) in summer to 18–27°C (64–81°F) in winter.

Left: *The southern coastline of Mauritius is largely deserted as it is not safe to swim along much of it, and the dive sites are all concentrated on Blue Bay.* Above: *Lagoons with rich coral growth harbour the Masked coachman.*

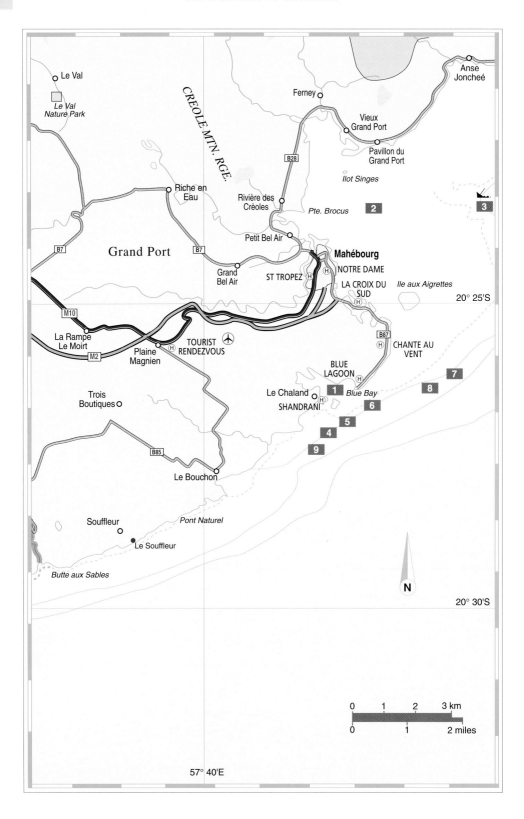

Le Val

Le Val
Nature Park

CRÉOLE MTN. RGE.

Ferney

Vieux
Grand Port

Anse
Jongheé

Pavillon du
Grand Port

B28

Riche en
Eau

Rivière des
Créoles

Ilot Singes

Pte. Brocus

2

3

Grand Port

B7

B7

Petit Bel Air

Grand
Bel Air

ST TROPEZ

Mahébourg

NOTRE DAME

LA CROIX DU
SUD

Ile aux Aigrettes

20° 25'S

M10

La Rampe
Le Moirt

M2

Plaine
Magnien

TOURIST
RENDEZVOUS

B87

CHANTE AU
VENT

7

Trois
Boutiques

BLUE
LAGOON

Le Chaland

SHANDRANI

Blue Bay

1

6

8

5

4

9

B85

Le Bouchon

Souffleur

Pont Naturel

Le Souffleur

Butte aux Sables

N

20° 30'S

0   1   2   3 km

0   1   2 miles

57° 40'E

The popular dive sites in the South sub-region are:

1 BLUE BAY

★★★ ☆ ☆ ☆ ☆ ☆ ☆

Location: Directly in front of the Shandrani Hotel, approximately 200m (219yds) from the shoreline. See map.
Access: Usually by boat from either of the dive centres operating in the area, but can also be reached by swimming from the shore.
Conditions: Lagoon conditions – crystal-clear water with visibility often exceeding 50m (164ft). There is no current and the site can be dived in virtually all weather conditions.
Average depth: 7m (23ft)
Maximum depth: 10m (33ft)

There must surely be very few divers who are not impressed by the strange and dramatic shapes that Nature has created for the many coral varieties that can be found in places like Blue Bay – perhaps only those divers whose fascination has been blunted by familiarity. There are plate corals (*Leptoseris* sp.), huge brain corals (*Platygyra daedalea*), staghorn corals (*Symphyllia valenciennesi* and *Acropora* spp.) and cabbage corals that, in some places, stand nearly 2m (6.6ft) high.

On this dive, nothing is constant as the diver is treated to a changing and varied landscape with each sweep of his or her flippers.

Although one's first impression is that there are few fish about, be patient: there is a wide range of fish species, many of which are still juvenile, including damselfish, butterflyfish, surgeonfish (well represented by the ubiquitous Moorish idols, *Zanclus cornutus*, who rove the lagoon in groups of two and three), and juvenile Sailfin tangs (*Zebrasoma veliferum*).

Cornetfish (*Fistularia petimba*) often gather in small groups, looking like large sticks hanging in the water, quietly watching you with their big eyes. Trumpetfish (*Aulostomus valentini*), or Flutemouths as they are also known, swim stoically past – only the gentle rippling of their symmetrical dorsal and anal fins gives any indication that they are moving.

This is a dive that will interest the curious and those who want to enjoy a peaceful dive in a fascinating and luxurious environment.

Because the water is so shallow in places and the coral gardens so easily accessible from the shore, it is possible to snorkel in much of Blue Bay. As you gently float on the sea's surface, constantly changing vistas open up before you and this is enormously absorbing.

At the time of writing Blue Bay is being researched with a view to having it declared as Mauritius's first official marine park.

2 TROU MOUTOU

★★

Location: The dive site is situated in the lagoon just north of the La Croix du Sud Hotel. See map.
Access: By boat from either of the diving centres operating in the subregion.
Conditions: Lagoon conditions similar to Blue Bay (No.1.).
Average depth: 7m (23ft)
Maximum depth: 10m (33ft)

This dive takes place where the coral reef gives way to the Mahébourg Channel, a deep-water channel that leads to the pass through the barrier reef opening to the sea. It is the waterway that ships used when Grand Port was the island's main harbour. The dive begins on a sandy floor and then moves to various outcrops of reef. As you make your way across the sand, keep a careful lookout for sand-coloured Scribbled pipefish (*Corythoichthys intestinalis*), seahorses (*Hippocampus* sp.) and Milk-soles (*Pardachirus marmoratus*). Divers are accompanied by a cloud of Sergeant-majors, a few Checkerboard wrasses (*Halichoeres hortulanus*) and juvenile trumpetfish and cornetfish. On reaching the coral reef, the divemaster usually feeds the fish. While this takes place the cloud thickens as more and more damselfish appear from out of the blue. It is fascinating to watch the anemonefish, who find themselves caught in a dreadful dilemma: on the one hand they want to defend their territory against the gathering intruders; on the other they want to grab their share of food as it falls to the floor of the sea. So they have a frenetic time – rushing one way to try and catch a piece of food as it passes by and then rushing back to see that no other fish have invaded their territory. All in all this is an interesting, relaxed and fun dive and one that is certainly worth doing if you are on the spot.

3 LE *SIRIUS* WRECK

★★★★

Location: The remains of the ship are located in the Mahébourg Channel at a place called Le Petit Pâte, which is midway between the isle of Mouchoir Rouge and Bois des Amourettes. See map.
Access: By boat from either of the dive centres operating in the subregion.
Conditions: The wreck lies in a bed of fine silt brought down by rivers, that have drained into Grand Port since the dawn of time. Because of the influence of these rivers visibility is never very good and when the silt is disturbed, it rapidly diminishes to almost nothing.
Average depth: 18m (59ft)
Maximum depth: 25m (82ft)

On 25 August 1810, during the naval battle of Mahébourg, the English warship H.M.S. *Sirius* was gutted by its officers and men when the ship ran aground. The ship burned for several hours before the flames reached its powder store, and then it was ripped apart in the ensuing explosion. Today three distinct sections have been identified: the front section, which lies at a depth of 10-12m (33-39ft) and is totally embedded in mud; the central section, which stretches from the foremast to the mizzenmast, is about 22m (72ft) long and lies at a depth of 16-22m (52-72ft); and a large pile of cannon balls has been found in the wreckage, no doubt marking the position where the ammunition was stored, which in turn denotes the position of the mainmast. The stern lies at 21-24m (69-79ft) and is located some 25m (82ft) away, indicating the force of the explosion.

Observations made by Yann von Arnim (marine biologist, chairman of the Mauritius Marine Conservation Society and amateur, but highly respected, maritime archaeologist living in Mauritius) on the influence the wreck has had on the marine environment, as reported in the MSDA's publication, *Caretta* (No. 2) 1990, makes very interesting reading:

'The presence of the fine silt, continuously discharged by the neighbouring rivers, has kept the wooden structures in perfect condition. This silt has completely buried the wreck, sheltering it from oxygen, the main element responsible for chemical degradation (wood rotting, oxidation of metal).

'All parts found outside the silt (cannons, hull, wood...) have rapidly become the shelter of many marine species, thus transforming this wreck into a really extraordinary ecological oasis in an almost barren ecosystem. Actually, moving down along the reef of the "Petit Pâte" on the way to the *Sirius*, a striking ecological contrast is revealed to the diver.

'The coral life gradually fades away from a depth of 10 metres onwards to give way to the silt apparently empty of any marine animals, but soon with the appearance of the first structures of the wreck, there is a whole fauna as varied as it is important.

'The ship is literally invaded by white whip-like coral, hence deserving the name of "white-haired" wreck. This coral constitutes a shelter for a multitude of small trumpet fish which live in close association with other fish like the redbreasted wrasse locally called "Madame Tombe" (*Cheilinus fasciatus*), schools of striped-eel catfish (*Plotosus lineatus*), blue-line snappers (*Lutjanus kashmira*), Giant trevally (*Caranx ignobilis*) and moorish idols (*Zanclus canescens*), all of which illuminate this gloomy and quiet scenery.

'The cannons constitute the realm of the invertebrates. Sponges, anemones, corals, bryozoans, hydrozoans, gasteropods, bivalves, nudibranches [*sic*] and ascidians squabble over the small quantities of substratum offered by the solid structure of the wreck. Here, a crayfish having made a shelter out of a piece of hull; there, an octopus living under a cannon, fortifying its shelter with a multitude of bottle and earthenware fragments. Its tentacles, with its suckers withdrawn, only let out its strangely expressive eyes: "Beware intruder! You are in my realm!"

'... This warship, once built to kill, slowly ends her career by giving life.'

4 GROTTE LANGOUSTE
★★★

Location: On the outside of the reef, off Ile des Deux Cocos, just to the north of the pass south of the Shandrani Hotel. See map.

Access: By boat from either of the dive centres. The journey takes less than 10 minutes.

Conditions: Situated outside the reef, the dive is subject to the vagaries of weather, and can become particularly tricky in winter. However, because of its relative proximity to the reef, where the general depth is around 20m (66ft), it is fairly well protected and can be dived throughout the year. Visibility averages between 20 and 25m (66-82ft), but on a good day can reach 50m (164ft).

Average depth: 21m (69ft)
Maximum depth: 23m (75ft)

This dive takes place in very broken terrain. It begins by proceeding through an archway that opens into a funnel and leads on to a sizable cavern that is full of large crayfish. The dive continues through this cavern and exits through a large hole. Depending on the direction of the current – if there is one – and the experience of the divers, it is possible to swim along a wall to Le Tunnel (No. 5. below), about 50m (164ft) away.

5 LE TUNNEL
★★★

Location: The site is located some 50m (164ft) southeast of Grotte Langouste. See map.

Access: By boat from either of the diving centres.

Conditions: The same as for Grotte Langouste (No. 4.).

Average depth: 21m (69ft)
Maximum depth: 23m (75ft)

The site has the same general site characteristics as Grotte Langouste. The attractiveness of this dive, however, lies in its 30m tunnel (98ft), through which the dive proceeds. It is important to take a powerful torch along so that you may have an opportunity to study the marine life that exists in the tunnel, a notable feature of which is the many crayfish that come out of their holes to see who these strange creatures are, passing through their territory. The dive is either done alone, or combined with No. 4. (above).

6 PURPLE CAVE

★ ★ ★

Location: Situated beyond the reef, on the northern side of the pass. See map.

Access: By boat from either of the diving centres serving the area.

Conditions: The same as for dive site No. 4. (page 112), except that it is more exposed to the open sea and therefore cannot be dived as frequently, particularly in winter.

Average depth: 18-20m (59-66ft)

Maximum depth: 21m (69ft)

Why this cave is called Purple Cave is a mystery, because it is festooned with *pink* corals. It is a large cave and can comfortably accommodate 20 divers. It houses lots of crayfish and eels within its cracks and crevices. Shoals of kingfish are frequent visitors to the cave and occasionally Black-tip sharks (*Carcharhinus melanopterus*) make an appearance. After the cave, the dive continues along the drop-off and into a long canyon which can be followed for some way, depending on what your computer tells you!

LIFE IN THE LAGOON

In addition to a wide range of coral species, the following can be seen in the lagoons of Mauritius:

Scissor-tail sergeant fish (*Abudefduf coelestinus*)
Teardrop butterflyfish (*Chaetodon unimaculatus*)
Blacktail damselfish (*Ascyllus melanurus*)
Stonefish (*Synanceia verrucosa*)
Spotfin scorpionfish (*Pterois antennata*)
Sea cucumber (Holothuroidea)
Striped squirrelfish (*Adioryx cornutus*)
Cross-hatch butterflyfish (*Chaetodon xanthurus*)
Chaine moray eel (*Echidna catenata*)
Long-spined sea urchin (*Echinidea* sp.)
Picasso triggerfish (*Rhinecanthus aculeatus*)
Tentacle mouth (Holothuroidea)
Threadfin butterflyfish (*Chaetodon auriga*)
Blue-green damselfish (*Chromis caerulea*)
White-eyed moray eel (*Siderea grisea*)
Cleaner wrasse (*Labroides dimidiatus*)
Green parrotfish (*Scarus sordidus*)
Sea razor blade (*Pinna* sp.)
Scaled pigmy angelfish (*Centropyge vroliki*)
Bicolor damselfish (*Chromis dimidiatus*)
Honeycomb grouper (*Epinephelus merra*)
One-spot snapper (*Lutjanus fulviflamma*)
Short-spined sea urchin (Cidaridae)
Moorish idol (*Zanclus canescens*)

7 COLORADO

★ ★ ★ ★ ★

Location: The dive site is located some 500-600m (547-656yds) beyond the barrier reef, opposite the remains of the wreck of the *Dalbair*, which sticks up quite prominently on the reef between the Shandrani and La Croix du Sud hotels. See map.

Access: By boat from either of the dive centres operating in the subregion.

Conditions: The dive site is further out to sea than the others in this area, and because it is deeper, it is more vulnerable to the moods of the sea and is entirely weather-dependent. When the wind blows the sea is normally too rough to dive and at other times there is a strong current that makes diving here both risky and unpleasant.

Average depth: 33m (108ft)

Maximum depth: 40m (131ft). (This applies to the dive area, but the canyon itself goes much deeper as it is part of the drop-off.)

The dive site gets its name from Colorado, home of America's Grand Canyon, which is one of the wonders of the world. This is a mini-grand canyon of the sea. Here the drop-off splits open to form a meandering canyon which is at least 400m (437yds) long and has steep rock faces, jagged cliffs and walls of giant rocks.

In the canyon turtles, tuna, kingfish, parrotfish, groupers, Sailfish (*Istiophorus gladius*), and parrotfish can be seen, while both Hammerhead and Black-tip reef sharks (*Carcharhinus melanopterus*) have been spotted, but only in the early morning and late afternoon, giving rise to a local theory that this is a nocturnal resting place for these roaming predators of the sea.

The dive proceeds down the canyon for a short distance and then enters a long, crayfish-filled tunnel (bring a torch), which twists and turns before exiting into a short chimney. As you pass through the chimney the scene opens onto a large amphitheatre, partially decked by a dramatic arch above you. You glide under this arch and turn through a narrow gorge which takes you back to the canyon – to a place that is a veritable forest of sea fans. Sadly, there isn't time to take more than a passing look at these magnificent gorgonians with their interesting shapes. The dive seems to pass in an instant and the long process of decompression begins ... but you will feel content because you have had a moment to look through one of God's windows.

Even if underwater speleology is not your idea of fun, don't dismiss this dive or be put off by the prospect of going through the tunnel. Hold onto your buddy if you are nervous – the rest of the dive will more than compensate for that moment of fear. There is so much to see during this dive, which is, unfortunately, a short one because of its depth.

Schools of Striped eel-catfish are common on or near the 19th-century wreck of the British Warship, Sirius.

This is a dive that you can do often without becoming bored – particularly if you are able to time your visit for the early morning or late afternoon when the fish life iis more active – earning this dive site a very well-deserved five-star rating.

8 ROCHES ZOZO

★★★★★

Location: This site is situated near Colorado (No. 7.). See map.
Access: By boat from either of the dive centres in the area.
Conditions: The same as for dive site No. 4. (page 112), except that it is more exposed to the open sea and therefore cannot be dived as frequently, particularly in winter.
Average depth: 33m (108ft)
Maximum depth: 40m (131ft)

Roches Zozo, or Bird Rock as it is known in English, is a pinnacle of rock that rises up from the floor of the sea to reach a point about 12m (39ft) below the surface of the water. Local fishermen named the site for the birds that gather there from time to time when shoals of fish come into the area.

The dive begins at this rocky outcrop and descends the face of the rock, which is lined with small caves and crevices containing an assortment of small corals and other marine organisms. While these are interesting in their diversity, they are limited in number.

At around 20m (66ft) there is a large plateau which leads to a tunnel into which the dive proceeds. This tunnel leads to a parallel canyon through which the dive

passes and continues to the opposite wall where there is a second tunnel that twists up and back on itself into the same canyon, only a little higher up, and directly beneath a huge arch which spans the canyon. From there it is back to the surface.

Both Roches Zozo and Colorado (No. 7.) are unusual dive sites that take place in dramatic and unusual scenery, which is the reason for their high star ratings – not the possibility of seeing large and exciting marine animals. The likelihood of seeing these at Roches Zozo is less than at Colorado, but for both dives, they should be considered an added bonus.

9 HAROLD'S POINT

★★

Location: Opposite the pass through the barrier reef south of Ile des Deux Cocos. See map.
Access: By boat from either dive centre in the subregion.
Conditions: As for Roches Zozo (No. 8.), this dive site, because of its position, is vulnerable to sea conditions. Therefore, rough windy seas and a strong current often make diving unpleasant and risky.
Average depth: 35m (115ft)
Maximum depth: 45m (148ft)

Again this is a dive done in broken terrain. Its outstanding feature is a huge archway under which a variety of fish congregate, particularly various species of grouper. It is an interesting dive and one worth doing if you are on the spot. However, due to the dive's great depth it is only suitable for qualified and experienced divers.

The South: Regional Directory

DIVING COSTS

The cost of a dive ranges from Rs600 to Rs900 for a night-dive outside the reef. A night-dive inside the reef costs Rs700. Full courses cost Rs5000 (CMAS), Rs7000 (NAUI) and a resort course costs Rs1200.

DIVING CENTRES

Diving in the south is concentrated in the Mahébourg/Blue Bay area in the southwest corner of this subregion.

From Blue Bay to Le Morne in the southwest subregion, there is no organized diving due to the nature of the coastline and sea, so no diving facilities exist for tourists along this sector of the Mauritian seaboard.

At present there are two diving centres which operate in the South.

They are:

• **Coral Dive Centre**,
La Croix du Sud, Mahébourg.
Tel: 631-9605 Fax: 631-9603

Coral Dive operates from the resort hotel La Croix du Sud at Mahébourg. The centre has Cressi-Sub equipment and can fully kit out 12 divers.

Coral Dive operates a 7m (23ft) Buccaneer semi-rigid, powered by twin 60HP Yamaha engines. The centre is affiliated to CMAS and offers training from a basic introductory course to a CMAS Two-Star certificate. Night dives are available on special request.

• **Shandrani Diving Centre**,
Shandrani Hotel, Blue Bay.
Tel: 637-3511 Fax: 637-4313

This dive centre operates from the grounds of the luxurious Shandrani Hotel at Blue Bay. The centre has Scubapro equipment and can kit out 10 divers, but dives are normally limited to five divers only. Shandrani Diving Centre has 12-litre steel and aluminium tanks. It operates two boats: a 16ft Catamaran with 50HP motors for use on dive sites located outside the reef and a 14ft monohull with a 40HP motor for use inside the lagoon.The centre is both CMAS and NAUI affiliated and

offers a basic introductory training course as well as either CMAS One-Star or NAUI Open Water One.

SPORT AND RECREATIONAL ACTIVITIES

Watersports

Water-skiing, windsurfing, yachting, kayaking, riding in a *pedalo*, parasailing and trips in a fibreglass-bottomed boat are offered by the beach hotels operating in this subregion. Speedboat trips and catamaran cruising are also available at a nominal fee.

All resort hotels have swimming pools around which residents can laze if they prefer to avoid the beach sand. A fun thing to do is to hire mountain bikes from the hotel and to cycle to the different beaches in the area, or, if you are feeling energetic, up into the beautiful Bambous mountains.

Alternatively you can explore along the coastal road.

Social games

Most beach hotels have tennis and volleyball courts, and indoor snooker rooms and board games for those who would like to escape the sunshine.

PLACES OF INTEREST

Mahébourg is the principal town of the southern part of the island. The town was established by General Decaen in 1806 to replace Vieux Grand Port, which was where the Dutch first landed and built a small settlement.

The town, which was named after Mahé de Labourdonnais, is situated across the harbour. For a brief period, between 1806 and 1801, it was known as Port Imperial, in honour of Emperor Napoléon Bonaparte.

An interesting few hours can be spent at the **Naval Museum** in Mahébourg where a room has been dedicated to the Battle of Grand Port, Napoléon's only naval victory, which took place on the tranquil waters of Grand Port Bay. The bell of the *St Géran* and a few other interesting relics are also on display at the museum.

A pleasant day can also be spent motoring down to **Le Morne**, along the island's south coast.

This is Mauritius's wild coast; for much of the coastline here the sea is not held back by a coral reef and instead it crashes into the cliffs that line its shore, cutting them back in places to form blow-holes – natural arches and bridges, some of which can be seen at Le Souffleur. From Souillac to Le Morne the road hugs the coastline and there are some lovely views to see and places to stop at and snorkel.

An interesting diversion on the return trip is to go to **Chamarel**, where there is a restaurant with a magnificent view over the whole of the southwest corner of the island, and a small area of **coloured earths** which is a natural wonder well worth seeing.

EATING OUT

The beach hotels operating in the South, as in much of Mauritius, structure their tariffs on a dinner, bed and breakfast basis and therefore tourists staying at these hotels usually have their meals at the hotel.

Lunches are available from the individual hotel's coffee shops or restaurants at extra cost, of course.

There are no restaurants in the immediate vicinity of Mahébourg that can be recommended and therefore it will be necessary to explore further afield to eat out (see previous subregions).

At Domaine du Chasseur in the Bambous mountains there is a small but interesting restaurant set high up in one of the valleys of this hunting reserve and nature park.

For those who want to go further, there are two restaurants on Ile aux Cerfs near Le Touessrok Hotel. **Paul et Virginie** restaurant is on the beach and specializes in seafood while **La Chaumière** is built on a lower hillside and specializes in Creole cooking. This restaurant is set in an attractive, jungle-like environment with thatched individual dining platforms built into the trees.

Both restaurants are only open between noon and 15:00.

Cowries
(Cypraeidae)

There are over 160 species of cowries (or porcelain shells). The cowrie has a colourful and glossy egg-like shape with an aperture that is made up of a narrow slit running the full length of the shell with both lips ridged or toothed.

Because it resembles the human female reproductive organ, the cowrie has enjoyed a special status amongst many tribal people as it was believed to ensure human fertility. When the animal is alive the shell is completely enclosed by the two folds of its mantle. These folds extend from the aperture and meet over the back, and it is this that protects the shell from wear and tear. When disturbed, this mantle retracts and reveals the glossy shell.

Cowries are grazers, living on sponges and small coral animals and feeding mainly at night. They reproduce by laying eggs which look like small capsules 'gummed' together and hidden under rocks. There the female cowrie will brood over her eggs in a hen-like manner.

The money cowrie was used as currency by the ancient Egyptians until the Greeks introduced metal discs. When the Chinese introduced metal coins into their currency in 600BC, they were, interestingly, shaped like cowries. The use of cowries as money persisted on the African continent until late into the 19th century. In west Africa cowries were threaded onto leather string, and transported over vast distances to pay for gold, slaves, palm oil and ivory. Slaves varied in price from 20,000 to 45,000 shells, while 60,000 to 100,000 shells would be needed as a dowry for a beautiful young wife. Cowries were also used to decorate shrines and figurines in the ancient Nigerian cities of Benin and Ife, and they were inlaid into the decorations of important buildings and the pavements surrounding them. In Ghana they were woven into the headresses of important chiefs. These cowries were collected in the seas and on the beaches of West Africa, and then transported to East Africa by camel across the deserts that lie inbetween. This 'added value' made cowries a very valuable currency in the markets of Timbuktu, Kano, Togo, Takoradi and in the Niger Delta.

Common cowrie species found in Mauritius are the Tiger, Carnelian, Arabic, and ring cowries.

Cone Shells
(Conidae)

Over 300 species of cone shells have been described to date. The cone family is identified by its consistent form: it resembles an inverted cone, with a very long and narrow aperture and a sharp-edged outer lip. It is a 'solid' shell and very heavy for its size. The largest species reaches about 15cm (6in) in length. At the base of the cone is a spire which, in most cases, takes the form of a flattened disc, with each whorl almost covering the previous one so that the spiral nature of the shell is not easily perceived unless it is held at right-angles to the spire. There are two exceptions: the one is the very rare Glory of the Sea (*Conus gloriamanis*) and the other is the even rarer *C. clytospira*. There are only nine known specimens of the latter species in the world, at least one of which was found in Mauritius.

Cone shells are multicoloured and are composed of a porcelainous material which in living shells is covered by a yellowish-brown epidermis (periostracum), protecting the shell. It can be carefully removed to reveal the full beauty of the shell. Although cone shells are fairly widely distributed, from the Mediterranean to South Africa, it is in tropical waters where they are most numerous and their colours most striking. Most cones inhabit deeper waters and can be found hiding in holes and crevices in coral reefs. All are predatory, silently and slowly stalking their prey, which includes other shells, sea worms and small fish.

Cones are armed with a long and fleshy poisoned proboscis that can protrude well beyond the edge of the shell. These 'tongues' have a number of barbs or radular teeth, each with a venom gland at its base, which is used to penetrate and stun or paralyze prey before slowly consuming it.

There are five species of cones or cone shells which are known to cause severe and even fatal stings to human beings. These are: *C. aulicus*, *C. textile*, *C. marmoreus*, *C. tulipa*, and *C. geographus*. If these shells are not carefully handled, their sharp proboscis can become a deadly weapon, so it is advisable to treat all cone shells with utmost caution.

Harp Shells
(*Harpa* sp.)

The early 19th-century English conchologist and author, Perry, described the harp shell in his book *Conchology* (1811) as 'one of the most laboured of Nature's works, as they present to the eye many little circumstances of high finishing and painting, which an artist can by no means easily imitate, or convey to the mind by any laboured description whatever'.

The Harp shell belongs to a small but very beautifully marked and coloured group of shells found in tropical waters. The *Harpa ventricosa*, a deep vermilion only found in Mauritius, Ceylon and the Philippines, is the rarest. The Greater harp shell (*H. major*) is lighter in colour and relatively common in the Indo-Pacific region. The third species, *H. harpa*, has shades of yellow in its seven ribs, and is smaller and more pointed. It is only found in the eastern and central Pacific region.

Harp shells have never been abundant and divers are unlikely to ever see one on their dives in Mauritius, but there was a time when they could be caught on a line. Broderip, the English naturalist and traveller, wrote in 1830 of his visit to Mauritius where he saw troops garrisoned there fishing for harp and olive shells: 'It is the amusement of the place to watch over the trim apparatus of lines hung over some sand bank to tempt the various brilliant species of olives which there abound, or to wait for the more rare appearance of the harp shell, till the rich hues of its inhabitants are seen glowing through the clear water, in the rays of a tropical rising sun.'

Besides the *H. major* and the *H. ventricosa*, other harp shells found in Mauritius are the *H. amouretta* and the Double harp, or *H. costata*, which has double the number of ribs and is only found in Mauritius.

Murex Shells
(Muricidae)

Murex shells are mainly found in the tropics. Characteristic of some are their long, protective spines, and in others their spiky, fluted frills. They live in calm, sheltered waters with a muddy bottom, where they prey upon bivalves and other shells. After the fall of the Roman Empire, dye made from the shells was used by the Christian church and it gave rise to the official purple colour of the cardinal's robe.

A number of murexes are found in Mauritius including the large and handsome, triangular-shaped Branched murex which has a spiky, fluted exterior and a red-lined aperture. Mature specimens grow up to 20 or 30cm (8–12in) in length. Other triangular species include the Adustus murex, a small specimen that grows to a maximum length of 5cm (2in), the Endive murex and the Short-spined murex, which is unmistakable with its extremely long siphonal canal and rows of short blunt knobs (spikes). Among the long-spined murexes, the Indian Ocean murex and the Venus comb murex were once relatively common. Others found in Mauritius include the following: *M. nigrispinosus*, *M. trapa*, *M. tribulus*, *Haustellum haustellum*, *Chicoreus palmarosae*, *C. saulli*, *C. torrefactus*, *Pterynotus tripterus*, *P. elongatus*, and *P. bipinnatus*.

THE MARINE ENVIRONMENT

Mauritian Reefs and Reef Life

Mauritius is a volcanic island that is almost fully encircled by coral reefs. Only along the island's southern coast does the reef give way to an open sea, which breaks unhindered on the island's relatively steeply sloping shore. Here there is virtually no continental shelf and this, combined with the sea's turbulence and the infusion of fresh water from the rivers which discharge into the sea along this stretch of coastline, make the growth of coral reefs problematical.

The Nature of Corals and Reefs

Tropical reefs are built mainly from corals, which are primitive animals closely related to sea anemones. Most of the coral types that contribute to reef construction are colonial, which means that numerous individuals – polyps – come together to create what is essentially a single compound organism. The polyps produce calcareous skeletons; when thousands of millions of them are present in a single colony, they form large, stony (in fact, limestone) structures which build up as reefs.

What happens is that, when corals die, at least some of the skeleton remains intact, thus adding to the reef. Cracks and holes then fill with sand and the calcareous remains of other reef plants and animals, and gradually the whole becomes consolidated, with new corals growing on the surface of the mass. Thus only the outermost layer of the growing reef is alive.

Corals grow slowly, adding about 1-10cm (0.4-4in) growth in a year. Once over a certain age they are able to reproduce, releasing tiny forms that float freely among the plankton for a few weeks until settling to continue their growth on the reef.

The forms corals create as they grow vary enormously according to the species and to the place on the reef where it is growing. Colonies range in size from a few centimetres in diameter to giants measuring several metres across and many hundreds of years old. Some are branched or bushy, others tree-like, others in the form of plates, tables or delicate leafy fronds, and yet others are encrusted, lobed, rounded or massive.

Microscopic plants called zooxanthellae are of great importance to the growth and health of corals. These are packed in their millions into the living tissues of most reef-building corals (and of various other reef animals, such as Giant clams [Tridacna spp.]). Although reef corals capture planktonic organisms from the water, a significant amount of their food comes directly from the zooxanthellae. It is for this reason that the most prolific coral growths are in the shallow, well-lit waters that the zooxanthellae prefer.The presence of coral communities does not, in fact, necessarily lead to the development of thick deposits of reef limestone. This is the case, though, in Mauritius, which consists mainly of slabs of volcanic rock with a patchy veneer of corals.

Types of Reef

In most regions with large coral communities, the calcareous skeletons have built up to form a variety of different types of reef:

• fringing reefs
• patch reefs, banks and shoals
• barrier reefs
• atolls

Fringing Reefs
Fringing reefs occur in shallow water near to land. Typically they extend to depths of 15-45m (49-148ft), depending on factors such as the profile and depth of the seabed, and the clarity of the water.

Corals do not occur where rivers flow into the sea because the fresh water reduces the required salinity levels of the sea water for the corals to be able to grow. Instead the river estuaries support stands of mangroves – another significant marine ecosystem of enormous importance. Mangroves are a heterogeneous group of plants which have independently (since there is no systematic or taxonomic relationship linking them) evolved mechanisms which enable them to adapt to a normally hostile habitat. The outstanding feature of this habitat is

---

Sea goldies, Silver-streak goldies, Threadfin goldies, and Coral rockcod, as well as a Lemonfish, hiding behind a stand of soft coral, keep a watchful eye on the intruder in their realm.

that, being part of the intertidal zone, it is inundated with sea water at high tide. In order to cope with constant tidal flooding and the high salinity levels in the water, mangrove trees have developed special root systems, as well as the ability to exclude much of the salt content in the sea water that they absorb. Those salts that are absorbed are exuded in concentrated form through glands situated on the underside of the leaves. In Mauritius, perhaps the most notable mangroves are those which occur in the Black River estuary in the island's Southwest region.

Patch Reefs, Banks and Shoals

In theory, reefs can develop anywhere where the underlying rock has at some time been close enough to the surface for corals to become established and grow. Sea levels may have risen considerably since then, or other geological changes may have occurred to lower the depth of the bed beneath the surface; either way, there are many places where reefs exist as isolated mounds or hillocks on the seabed.

Patch reefs are found in relatively shallow waters around Mauritius. They vary in size, from a couple of metres in length to many hundreds of metres. In some parts of the world patch reefs stretching for a number of kilometres occur, often lying in deep waters with their tops rising to within 20m (66ft) of the surface. These are usually referred to as banks or shoals.

Barrier Reefs

Barrier reefs occur along the edges of islands or continental shelves, and are substantial structures. The major difference, apart from size, between them and fringing reefs is that they are separated from the shore by a wide, deep lagoon. The outer edge of the barrier drops away steeply to the ocean floor beyond. Initially these reefs formed in shallow waters; then, as sea levels increased, they built progressively upwards so that their living topmost parts were still near the surface of the water.

The coral reefs around Mauritius are often referred to as 'barrier reefs' because they provide a barrier between the lagoons and the open sea. Strictly speaking, however, this is not correct since barrier reefs, as already mentioned, are substantial, almost terrestrial structures. The best known example of a barrier reef is the Great Barrier Reef which occurs off Australia's east coast.

Atolls

Formations of ancient origin, atolls take the form of ring-shaped reefs enclosing shallow lagoons, and dropping away to deep water on their outsides. Atolls are initially formed as fringing reefs around volcanic islands, and they keep growing as the underlying base gradually subsides beneath the water level, although there is evidence that atolls may form for other reasons as well. Most of the world's atolls are in the Indian and Pacific oceans. Mauritius's offshore islands of Cargados Carajos, or the St Brandon archipelago, is made up of a group of 22 atolls.

Reef Life

Along the coral reefs and within the lagoons that surround Mauritius, there is a world of immense fascination. Staghorn corals (*Acropora* spp.), a spiky coral with many branches that resemble the antlers of a stag, is a fast growing coral and an early colonizer of disturbed areas. Plate coral (*Leptoseris* sp.) is very common and is made up of flat, plate-like sheets, some up to 1m (3ft) in diameter, which spread out in layers across the reef. Other typical corals include mushroom (*Fungia scutaria*), knob-horned (*Pocillopora verrucosa*), honeycomb (*Favites* spp.), brain (*Platygyra daedalea*), turbinate (*Turbinaria mesenterina*) and turret (*Denrophyllia aurea*) corals. For the most part, however, the corals of Mauritius are composed of a crust of hard and soft corals which cover the volcanic rocks that make up the ocean floor.

Fish life on coral reefs is another chapter of great interest to divers. There are herbivores (marine plant feeders), carnivores (those that feed on animals), and omnivores (those that eat both plants and animals). A wide variety of fish species is found in Mauritian waters, but being a subtropical island, the actual numbers seen on each dive are generally quite limited.

Large gorgonia sea fans are a common sight, especially in the deeper waters on the drop-off beyond these encircling coral reefs – in some places it is like swimming through a veritable forest.

Sponges of all colours grow on the coral cliffs and in the valleys created by volcanic rocks that are piled up on the seabed.

Sea urchins are relatively common; the slate pencil urchin (*Heterocentrotus mammillatus*), which has large, smooth and attractively banded spines is found in the deeper waters off-shore, while its cousin (*Diadema setosum*), which has long, needle-like spines, is found mainly in the lagoons and shallower waters.

Reef Zones and Habitats

Reefs can be divided into a number of zones reflecting differences in such features as depth, profile, distance from the shore, amount of wave action, and type of seabed. Associated with each zone are characteristic types of marine life.

The Lagoon

A lagoon fills the area between the shore and the seaward reef. Here the seabed is usually a mixture of sand, coral rubble, limestone slabs and living coral colonies. The water depth varies from a few metres to 50m (164ft) or more (in the north between the main island and Coin de Mire), and the size of the lagoon can be anywhere from a few hundred to thousands of square metres. The largest and deepest lagoons are generally associated with barrier reefs and atolls, and may be dotted with islands and smaller reefs.

Sites within lagoons are obviously more sheltered than those on the seaward reef, and are also more affected by sedimentation. Here there are many attractive seaweeds. Most of the corals are delicate, branching types. Large sand-dwelling anemones are often found in lagoons and, in places, soft corals and 'false corals' are likely to form mats over the seabed. Especially where there is a current you may encounter extensive beds of seagrasses, the only flowering plants to occur in the sea. Among the many animals that make these pastures their home are sea cucumbers.

Although some typical reef fishes are absent from the lagoon environment, there is no shortage of interesting species such as the roving predators – snappers, wrasses, triggerfish, emperors and others – on the lookout for worms, crustaceans, gastropods, sea urchins and small fish. Then there are the bottom-dwelling fishes that burrow into the sand, emerging only to feed.

Most entertaining to watch – if you spot them – are the small gobies that live in association with Pistol shrimps. In this partnership the shrimp is the digger and the goby, stationed at the entrance to the burrow, is the sentry. The small fish remains ever on the alert, ready to retreat hurriedly into the burrow at the first sign of disturbance. The shrimp has very poor eyesight; it keeps its antennae in close touch with the goby so that it can pick up the danger signal and, likewise, retire swiftly to the safety of the burrow.

The Reef Flat
Reef flats do not occur in Mauritius as there is no large intertidal zone, due to the topography of the island. Reef flats are formed as their associated reefs push steadily seaward, leaving behind limestone areas that are eroded and planed almost flat by the action of the sea. The reef flat is essentially an intertidal area, but at high tide it can provide interesting snorkelling.

The Seaward Reef Front
In Mauritius virtually all scuba diving takes place on the reef front, because this is where the deeper waters lie and where spectacular features and impressive displays of marine life are found. Brightly lit, clean, plankton-rich water provides ideal growing conditions for corals, and the colonies they form help create habitats of considerable complexity.

There is infinite variety, from shallow gardens of delicate branching corals to walls festooned with soft corals and sea fans.

The top 20m (66ft) or so of the seaward reef is especially full of life. Here small, brilliantly coloured damselfish and anthias swarm around the coral, darting into open water to feed on plankton.

Butterflyfish show their dazzling arrays of spots, stripes and intricate patterns as they probe into crevices or pick at coral polyps – many have elongated snouts especially adapted for this delicate task, such as the Moorish idol (Zanclus canescens) which scans the reefs, usually in pairs, but occasionally in threesomes.

By contrast, you can see parrotfish biting and scraping at the coral, over time leaving their characteristic white scars. Open-water species like fusiliers and snappers cover quite large areas when feeding, and wrasses often forage far and wide over the reef. But many species are more localized and can be highly territorial, on occasion even being prepared to take on a trespassing diver.

Clownfishes (Amphiprion spp.), or anemonefish, are among the boldest of the little fish, dashing out from the safety of anemone tentacles to give chase to those who venture too close.

Fish-watching can provide a diver with endless pleasure, but there is much else to see. Any bare spaces created on the reef are soon colonized, and in some places the surface is covered with large organisms that may be tens or even hundreds of years old.

These sedentary reef-dwellers primarily rely on, aside from the omnipresent algae, water-borne food. Corals and their close relatives – anemones, sea fans and black corals – capture planktonic organisms using their tiny stinging cells.

Sea squirts and sponges strain the plankton as seawater passes through special canals in their body-walls. Other organisms have different techniques: the Christmastree worm, for example, filters out food with the aid of its beautiful feathery 'crown' of tentacles.

Apart from the fishes and the sedentary organisms there is a huge array of other life forms to observe on the reef. Tiny crabs live among the coral branches and larger ones wedge themselves into appropriate nooks and crannies, often emerging to feed at night. Spiny lobsters hide in caverns, coming out to hunt under cover of darkness. Gastropod molluscs are another type of marine creature seldom seen during the day, but they are in fact present in very large numbers, especially on the shallower parts of the reef; many of them are small, but on occasion you might come across one of the larger species, like the Giant triton (Charonia tritonis).

Some of the most easily spotted of the mobile invertebrates are the echinoderms. Most primitive of these are the feather stars, sporting long delicate arms in all colours from bright yellow to green, red and black. The best known of their relatives, the sea urchins, is the black, spiny variety that lives in shallow reef areas and is a potential hazard to anyone walking onto the reef.

Many of the small, brightly coloured starfish that wander over the reef face feed on the surface film of detritus and micro-organisms.

Others are carnivorous, browsing on sponges and sea mats, and a few feed on living coral polyps. The damage they cause depends on their size, their appetite and, collectively, their population density. Potentially the most damaging of all is the large predator, the Crown-of-Thorns starfish (Acanthaster planci) (see feature on page 58 for further details).

Whether brilliantly attractive or frankly plain, whether swift or sessile, all the life forms you find on the reef are part of its finely balanced ecosystem. Divers are intruders: make it your obligation to cause as little disturbance and destruction in this wonderland as possible.

Marine Conservation in Mauritius

Over the last three decades divers in Mauritius have noted, with great concern, the diminishing marine resources of the island and the widespread death of corals. Marine biologists working with divers have been able to identify some of the causes and practices which reduce the productivity of the marine environment. The following has been noted:

• The frequent use of explosives in the past to harvest fish has destroyed many reef ecosystems and it is an ineffective and highly wasteful way of fishing.

• There has been a dramatic increase in the pollution of coastal waters by river-borne refuse, sewerage outfalls and waste from fishing boats. At the time of writing, for example, divers are monitoring the high levels of pollution caused, inter alia, by sewerage outfalls in the Péreybère area of the North subregion.

• Considerable damage is caused to corals by the use of anchors by diving and fishing boats anchored on the reefs, by local snorkellers removing specimens for sale to tourists, and by souvenir hunting by tourists themselves.

• The wholesale removal of sand for building destroys an important lagoon ecosystem and has caused the erosion of beaches. At the time of writing this practice is particularly noticeable in the Mahébourg area.

• Indiscriminate spear-fishing and collecting of shells has made the coastal waters less attractive to tourists and resident divers, and less productive as a source of food.

• The increasing use of lagoons for recreation and tourism has considerably reduced the pristine nature of the shoreline and coast.

• Disturbance by motor boats, fishermen and divers all play a part in decreasing the quality of the marine environment.

• Whales, dolphins and turtles are being harassed or even killed.

• Areas officially gazetted as fishing reserves are still being fished and government regulations are not observed. Indeed it has been noted that existing legislation, which forbids the use of explosives, spear-fishing, collecting of corals and shells, and fishing in some areas and during certain periods, appears to be difficult to enforce.

In order to help address these issues divers, through their organized association – the Mauritius Underwater Group – brought into being the Mauritius Marine Conservation Society (MMCS), a nonprofit organization dedicated to the conservation of the marine environment of Mauritius. (The aims and objectives of the society have been described in 'Diving and Snorkelling in Mauritius' on page 25.) The Society has set itself the dual task of monitoring marine environmental stress and lobbying government for its effective amelioration, and of demonstrating the benefits of marine conservation to the public while enlisting public support for government conservation measures.

Since its formation the Mauritius Marine Conservation Society has undertaken a number of successful projects (see page 122 for details).

Artificial reefs play an important part in marine development and conservation. Over the centuries fishermen have increased their yields by creating reefs (that could be either fixed or floating) in a waterbody in order to attract aquatic life which uses the reef for shelter, attachment, navigation orientation, spawning and feeding.

In some countries the creation of artificial reefs has become an industrial process. In Japan, for example, nearly US$1 billion will have been spent in the period 1981 to 1995 to create artificial reefs. Considerable expertise has been developed in the design and construction of fish aggregating devices (FADs) which are suitable for the coastal and fishing conditions of that country.

The USA has likewise spent millions on creating artificial reefs. Particular use has been made of waste materials (building waste, tyres, vehicles and old ships).

In Mauritius 15 FADs have been installed around the coast since 1986 and, as previously mentioned, the MMCS has sunk nine ships in coastal waters at varying depths (24-63m) (79-207ft).

Although much is still unknown about artificial reefs and the nature of their effect on marine growth, international research done so far indicates that inshore artificial reefs provide feeding, breeding and shelter functions, whereas pelagic artificial reefs primarily provide navigation and feeding functions. Therefore it does appear that localized enhancement of productivity can occur in shallower coastal areas, whereas in the pelagic zone, artificial reefs are more likely to play a concentrating role – certainly as far as fish are concerned.

This chapter is based on a paper presented by Philippe La Hausse de Lalouvierre of the Mauritius Marine Conservation Society at a Rotary International Seminar 'Protéger la planète Terre' held on 21 March 1991 at the Maritim Hotel, Mauritius.

DATE	NAME OF VESSEL	SITE	STRUCTURE	DEPTH
30.08.80	Water Lily	Trou aux Biches	Barge & tyres	24m (79ft)
23.05.81	Emily	Troux aux Biches	Barge & tyres	24m (79ft)
14.11.81	Tug 11	Flic en Flac	Tug & tyres	20m (66ft)
10.05.87	St Gabriel	Troux aux Biches	Cargo ship	38m (125ft)
11.10.87	Kei Sei 113	Troux aux Biches	Trawler	36m (118ft)
06.12.87	Stella Maru	Trou aux Biches	Trawler	22m (72ft)
03.12.89	Carp	Le Morne	Cargo ship	63m (207ft)
27.12.92	Silver Star	Grand Baie	Fishing ship	38m (125ft)
25.07.93	L'Orient	Flic en Flac	Fishing ship	40m (131ft)

To date the MMCS has been responsible for the creation of nine artificial reefs through the sinking of the vessels listed above.

The MMCS has done extensive evaluaton of its artificial reefs: each ship has been monitored from the date of its sinking, with the exception of one – the Carp – which is too deep. What has been revealed so far is that, in the case of the wrecks at Trou aux Biches, and Tug II at Flic en Flac, an oasis of marine life has been successfully created in each area – areas which were sand flats previously devoid of fish life. Observations in all cases revealed that, within weeks of sinking, each ship attracted pelagic fish. All wrecks now harbour species of resident benthic reef fishes, as well as crustacean, mollusc and algal species. All but the St Gabriel and the Kei Sei 113 have been colonized by a variety of hard and soft coral species (the suspected reason for these exceptions lies in the combination of depth and position of the sites). The wrecks themselves have been virtually covered in algal growth which provides a home for various populations of invertebrates. Artificial reefs in water deeper than 25m (82ft) tend to have less attached fauna than those in shallower water.

Artificial reefs have become popular fishing grounds for a number of local fishermen and those reefs easily accessible to dive centres have become popular wreck dive sites. This has meant that the MMCS's initial concept of creating 'mini-reserves' around each artificial reef has not been achieved and clearly indicates that without the necessary laws and law enforcement agency to back those laws, it is not possible to create marine reserves.

Mauritius has no marine reserves; admittedly it does have areas where net-fishing is prohibited in terms of official government notice (G.N. 18 of 1983 & G.N. 128 of 1984), but these areas fail to comply with the IUCN's World Conservation Strategy, which stipulates that for conservation to be effective it must preserve genetic diversity, maintain life-supporting ecosystems and provide for the sustainable utilization of natural resources. Conservationists in Mauritius have identified three obstacles to the achievement of marine parks on the island.

The first is the fact that protecting marine areas without the assurance of concomitant management of the adjoining terrestrial region is unlikely to result in a satisfactory long-term achievement. Secondly, the choice of the site and size of proposed reserves depends to a large degree on biological and hydrological data – information which is not readily available. Thirdly, government involvement is essential, especially in the provision of a legal framework for the establishment of marine parks and its enforcement. Neither of these exists at present. The MMCS is actively involved in addressing the problem at all three levels, because it is convinced that the creation of marine reserves is essential for the long-term survival of the country's marine ecosystems.

In conclusion, the general consensus is that the MMCS's artificial reef programme has been successful in creating new areas of biodiversity and these serve a positive function, especially for recreational diving. It is acknowledged that it would be unrealistic to expect that nine artificial reefs could have a measurable effect on productivity within the context of the 1020km^2 (634 sq miles) inshore shelf that surrounds Mauritius. It is also acknowledged that while the biological impact of these reefs has not yet been scientifically quantified, all observations suggest that the programme has been effective on a localized basis in this regard.

The creation of marine conservation areas which are protected from degradation is, in the view of MMCS, a logical extension of the artificial reef programme and similarly should be tackled on the basis of a series of small, manageable and replicable projects. The main deficiency of such an approach is that it treats some causes and effects rather than addresses all the causes of marine environmental degradation. However, Mauritian conservationists rightly argue that the great benefit of this approach is that, if successfully conducted, it mobilizes public (including legislators') attention and opinion, and this, in the final analysis, is what will make subsequent conservation activity more likely to be successful in conserving Mauritius's marine environment.

Diving and Conservation Organizations in Mauritius

Recompression Chamber

There is only one recompression chamber in Mauritius, situated at the headquarters of the paramilitary Special Mobile Force at Vacoas.

Mauritius Underwater Group

The Mauritus Underwater Group (MUG) was founded in 1964 for the express purpose of promoting the sport of diving in Mauritius. It is fully recognized by the Confédération Mondiale des Activités Subaquatiques (CMAS) or the World Underwater Federation and the British Sub Aqua Club (BSAC), and forms part of the Mauritius Scuba Diver's Association. The Group has a membership of about 100 enthusiasts and meets socially every Tuesday and Sunday night. MUG has two Bauer compressors and a limited amount of equipment for hire. Temporary membership is available for visitors to Mauritius, providing the applicant is a qualified diver, and this allows access to all of the club's facilities including the hire of equipment. MUG is housed in premises leased from the government situated in Railway Road, Phoenix.

Mauritius Marine Conservation Society

The Mauritius Marine Conservaton Society (MMCS) was formed in 1979 by a group of people whose interest in the marine environment developed from their association with the Mauritius Underwater Group. The MMCS was officially constituted and registered in May 1980 as a voluntary, nonprofit organization dedicated to the conservation of the marine environment of Mauritius. The MMCS is managed by a committee that is elected at the society's annual general meeting. It has its headquarters in the Mauritius Underwater Group's property in Phoenix. The objectives of the society are:

(a) To promote an awareness and appreciation of marine life and an interest in the need for marine conservation in Mauritius.

(b) To arouse an interest in the creation of marine parks to regenerate marine life and also to serve recreational and educational functions.

(c) To encourage the public and visitors to respect laws relating to all aspects of the protection of marine life, the marine environment and the preservation of underwater sites of archaeological interest and value to Mauritius.

(d) To induce government to enforce existing laws controlling spear-fishing, dynamite-fishing, shell and coral collection, net-fishing, aquatic pollution and the general destruction of the reefs.

The major tasks currently being undertaken by the Mauritius Marine Conservation Society include the following:

• To lobby for the prohibition of spear-fishing, shell and coral collecting, and fishing with explosives.

• To publicize the plight of natural reefs and to create sites for colonization by corals, algae, crustaceans and fish and to build artificial reefs by using appropriate materials, such as old ships, which has begun with the sinking of nine vessels. (See page 121.)

• To survey artificial reefs, using underwater video equipment.

• To make underwater videos of both pristine and damaged reef areas for public viewing.

• To present slide and video talks on marine conservation to schools, fishermen and the general public.

• To publish articles in the MMCS newsletter DIODON, as well as in local newspapers and magazines, and to publish books and posters on conservation and the marine environment.

• To work with other organizations to create marine parks through conferences and seminars on the subject.

• To conduct several Crown-of-Thorns starfish surveys.

• To conduct surveys of the occurrence and status of whales and dolphins in Mauritius.

• To promote conservation through publishing educational games for children with marine conservation themes, and running conservation essay competitions.

Membership of the Society is by subscription and besides having the opportunity to contribute to an organization which is active in lobbying against the ever-increasing threats to the marine environment, members receive DIODON free and other Society publications at a reduced cost; invitations to regular lectures, films and social events; and the opportunity to participate in expeditions and projects organized by the Society. For further information contact:

The Secretary, Mauritius Marine Conservation Society, c/o Mauritius Underwater Group, Railway Road, Phoenix, Mauritius (Tel: 696-5368).

UNDERWATER PHOTOGRAPHY AND VIDEO

Photography has become one of the most popular underwater pastimes. Being able to capture on film some of the amazing creatures we see underwater is highly rewarding, but can also prove incredibly frustrating, as the real difficulties of underwater photography – backscatter, fish that refuse to stay still, flooded camera housings and so on – become apparent. You need a lot of perseverance – and luck – to get really good results, but if you're prepared to persist you'll find you've developed a passion that will last for a lifetime of diving.

Shallow-Water Cameras
There are several cameras on the market that are suitable for snorkelling. Kodak and Fuji both offer cheap, single-use cameras that are waterproof down to about 2m (6.6ft) and work well enough in clear, sunlit waters. If you object to disposables, Minolta and Canon make slightly more expensive cameras that can be used down to depths of about 5m (16ft).

Submersible Cameras and Housings
You have essentially two main options for serious underwater photography. The first is to splash out on a purpose-built waterproof camera; the second is to buy a waterproof housing for your normal SLR or land camera. Each system has its pros and cons.

The submersible camera used by most professionals is the Nikonos, a 35mm non-reflex camera with TTL (through-the-lens) automatic exposure system and dedicated flashguns. (A popular alternative is the Sea & Sea Motor Marine II.) The specially designed Nikonos lenses give sharper results underwater than any of the housed lenses, but the lack of reflex focusing makes it difficult to compose pictures, and you can easily cut off part of a subject. They range from 15mm to 80mm in focal length, but must be changed above water. Underwater, the 35mm lens is of much use only with extension tubes or close-up outfits, though it can be used on land. The 28mm lens should be considered the standard.

Other companies supply accessories for the Nikonos: lenses, lens converters, extension tubes and housings to accommodate fish-eye and superwide land-camera lenses. Lens converters are convenient: they can be changed underwater. The Motor Marine II makes good use of these, with converters for wide-angle and macro.

The Nikonos close-up kit can also be changed underwater. Nikonos has recently introduced the RS-AF, a fully waterproof reflex camera with autofocus and dedicated lenses and flashgun, but it is extremely heavy and expensive. It is a poor buy in comparison with land cameras like Nikon's 801, F90 and F4 in housings; these are more versatile, weigh less, and can also be used on land.

Land cameras can be used underwater in specialist metal or plexiglass housings. Housings without controls, as used for fully automatic cameras, require fast films to obtain reasonable shutter speeds and lens apertures in the low ambient light underwater. Housings are available for all top-grade reflex cameras, but there are advantages and disadvantages to each system:
• Metal housings are strong, reliable, work well at depth and last a long time if properly maintained; they are heavier to carry, but are buoyant in water. Their higher cost is justified if your camera is expensive and deserves the extra protection.
• Plexiglass housings are fragile and need careful handling both in and out of the water; they are available for a wide range of cameras. They are lightweight, which is convenient on land, but in water are often too buoyant, so that you have to attach extra weights to them.
• Some models compress at depth, so the control rods miss the camera controls ... but, if you adjust the rods to work at depths, they do not function properly near the surface! However, as most underwater photographs are taken near the surface, in practice this drawback is not usually serious.

'O' Rings
Underwater cameras, housings, flashguns and cables have 'O' ring seals. These and their mating surfaces or grooves must be kept scrupulously clean. 'O' rings should be lightly greased with silicone grease to prevent flooding; too much grease will attract grit and hairs. Silicone spray should not be used, as the cooling can crack the 'O' ring. Removable 'O' rings should be stored off the unit to stop them becoming flat, and the unit itself should be sealed in a plastic bag to keep out moisture. User-removable 'O' rings on Nikonos cameras and flash-synchronization cables are best replaced every 12 months, and nonremovable ones every 12-18 months. 'O' rings usually last the life of the housing.

The Longfin batfish is common in tropical waters, but is an infrequent visitor to Mauritius.

Lighting

Sunlight can give spectacular effects underwater, especially in silhouette shots. When the sun is at a low angle, or in choppy seas, much of the light fails to penetrate the surface. To get the best of it, photograph two hours either side of the sun's highest point. Generally you should have the sun behind you and on your subject.

Water acts as a cyan (blue-green) filter, cutting back red, so photographs taken with colour film have a blue-green cast. Different filters can correct this in either cold or tropical waters, but they reduce the already limited amount of light available. The answer is flash, which will put back the colour and increase apparent sharpness.

Modern flashguns have TTL automatic-exposure systems. Underwater, large flashguns give good wide-angle performance up to 1.5m (5ft). Smaller flashguns have a narrower angle and work up to only 1m (3ft); diffusers widen the angle of cover, but you lose at least one f-stop in output. Some land flashguns can be housed for underwater use.

Flashguns used on or near the camera make suspended particles in the water light up like white stars in a black sky (backscatter); the closer these are to the camera, the larger they appear. The solution is to keep the flash as far as possible above and to one side of the camera. Two narrow-angle flashguns, one each side of the camera, often produce a better result than a single wide-angle flashgun. In a multiple-flash set-up the prime flashgun will meter by TTL (if available); any other flashgun connected will give its pre-programmed output, so should be set low to achieve modelling light.

When photographing divers, remember the eyes within the mask must be lit. Flashguns with a colour temperature of 4500K usually give more accurate skin tones and colour.

Fish scales reflect light in different ways depending on the angle of the fish to the camera. Silver fish reflect more light than coloured, and black fish almost none at all, so to make sure you get a good result you should bracket exposures. If using an automatic flashgun, do this by altering the film-speed setting. At distances under 1m (3ft) most automatic flashguns tend to overexpose, so allow for this.

The easiest way to balance flash with available light is to use TTL flash with a camera set on aperture-priority metering. Take a reading of the mid-water background that agrees with your chosen flash-synchronization speed, and set the aperture one number higher to give a deeper blue. Set your flash to TTL and it will correctly light your subject.

Film

Once you have learnt the correct exposures for different situations you can begin experimenting aesthetically with manual exposure. For b/w photography, fast 400 ISO film is best. For beginners wishing to use colour, negative print film is best as it has plenty of exposure latitude. (Reversal film is better for reproduction, but requires very accurate exposure.) Kodachrome films are ideal for close work but can give mid-water shots a blue-green water background; although this is in fact accurate, people are conditioned to a 'blue' sea. Ektachrome and Fujichrome produce blue water backgrounds; 50-100 ISO films present the best compromise between exposure and grain, and pale yellow filters can be used to cut down the blue.

Subjects

Subject depends on personal interest. Macro photography, with extension tubes and fixed frames, is easiest to get right: the lens-to-subject and flash-to-subject distances are fixed, and the effects of silting in the water are minimized. Expose a test film at a variety of exposures with a fixed set-up; the best result tells you the exposure to use in future for a particular setting and film.

Some fish are strongly territorial. Surgeonfish, triggerfish and sharks may make mock attacks; you can get strong pictures if you are brave enough to stand your ground. Manta rays are curious and will keep coming back if you react quietly and do not chase them. Angelfish and butterflyfish swim off when you first enter their territory, but if you remain quiet they will usually return and allow you to photograph them.

Diver and wreck photography are the most difficult. Even with apparently clear water and wide-angle lenses there will be backscatter, and you need to use flash if you are going to get a diver's mask to show.

Underwater night photography introduces you to another world. Many creatures appear only at night, and some fish are more approachable because they are half-asleep. However, focusing quickly in dim light is difficult, and many subjects disappear as soon as they are lit up, so you need to preset the controls.

On the Shoot – Tips

• Underwater photography starts before you enter the water. If you have a clear idea of your subject, you are likely to get better results. And, remember, you can't change films or prime lenses underwater!

• Autofocus systems that work on contrast (not infrared) are good underwater only for high-contrast subjects.

• When you are balancing flash with daylight, cameras with faster flash-synchronization speeds – 1/125sec or 1/250sec – give sharper results with fast-moving fish. The lens aperture will be larger, so focus must be accurate.

• Masks keep your eyes distant from the viewfinder. Buy the smallest-volume mask you can wear.

• Cameras fitted with optical action finders or eyepiece magnifiers are useful in housings but not so important with autofocus systems.

• Coloured filters can give surrealistic results, as do starburst filters when photographing divers with shiny equipment, lit torches or flashguns set to slave.

• Entering the water overweight makes it easier to steady yourself. Wearing an adjustable buoyancy lifejacket enables you to maintain neutral buoyancy.

• Remember not to touch coral and do not wear fins over sandy bottoms – they stir up the sand.

• Photographers do not swim around much, so wear a wetsuit for warmth.

• Refraction through your mask and the camera lens makes objects appear one-third closer and larger than in air. Reflex focusing and visual estimates of distances are unaffected but, if you measure a distance, compensate by reducing the resultant figure by one-third when setting the lens focus.

• When there is a flat port (window) in front of the lens, the focal length is increased and the image sharpness decreased due to differential refraction. Most pronounced with wide-angle lenses, this should be compensated for using a convex dome port.

Dome ports need lenses that can focus on a virtual image at about 30cm (12in), so you may have to fit supplementary +1 or +2 dioptre lenses.

Video

Underwater video photography is easier. Macro subjects require extra lighting but other shots can be taken using available light with, if necessary, electronic improvement afterwards. Backscatter is much less of a problem. You can play the results back on site and, if unhappy, have another try – or, at the very least, use the tape again somewhere else.

A major problem for travelling photographers and videographers is battery charging. AA or D cell batteries are available throughout Mauritius, particularly in Port Louis and Curepipe, but they may be old or have been badly stored – if the weight does not preclude this, it is best to carry your own spares.

Despite their memory problems, rechargeable nickel-cadmium batteries have advantages in cold weather, recharge flashguns much more quickly and, even if flooded, can usually be used again. Make sure you carry spares and that your chargers are of the appropriate voltage for your destination. Quick chargers are useful as long as the electric current available is strong enough. Most video cameras and many flashguns have dedicated battery packs, so remember to carry at least one spare and to keep it charged.

HEALTH AND SAFETY FOR DIVERS

The information in this section is intended as a guide only and is no substitute for thorough training or professional medical advice, nor is it intended to imitate a comprehensive manual on the subject.

The information is based on currently accepted health and safety advice. It is strongly advised that the reader obtain a recognized manual on diving safety and medicine before embarking on a trip.

Please note that:

• Divers who have suffered any diving-related injury or symptom of an injury, no matter how minor, should consult a doctor, preferably a specialist in diving medicine, as soon as possible after the symptom or injury occurs.

• If you are the victim of a diving injury, do not hesitate to reveal your symptoms no matter how minor they may seem to be. Mild symptoms can develop into a major illness with life-threatening consequences. It is better to be honest with yourself and live to dive another day.

• No matter how confident you are in formulating your own diagnosis, remember that unless you are a trained medical practitioner, *you are not a doctor.*

• Always err on the conservative side when considering your ailment: if you discover that your illness is only minor, the worst that can happen is that both you and your doctor will be relieved.

General Principles of First Aid

The basic principles of first aid include:
• DOING NO HARM
• SUSTAINING LIFE
• PREVENTING DETERIORATION
• PROMOTING RECOVERY

Safety

In the event of any illness or injury, a simple sequence of patient assessment and management can be followed. The sequence first involves assessment and definition of any life-threatening conditions followed by management of the problems found. The first things to check are commonly known as the ABCs, i.e.:

A. AIRWAY (with care of the neck)
B. BREATHING
C. CIRCULATION
D. DECREASED level of consciousness
E. EXPOSURE

Ensure both the patient's and your own safety by removing yourselves from the threatening environment (usually the water). Make sure that whatever your actions, they in no way further endanger the patient or yourself.

NEVER ASSUME THAT THE PATIENT IS DEAD.

Check the ABCs, as follows:

A. AIRWAY
1. With attention to the neck, is there a neck injury?
2. Is the mouth and the nose free of obstruction? Any noisy breathing is a sign of airway obstruction.

B. BREATHING
1. Look at the chest to see if it is rising and falling.
2. Listen for air movement at the nose and mouth.
3. Feel for the movement of air against your cheek.

C. CIRCULATION
1. Feel for a pulse next to the windpipe (carotid artery).

D. DECREASED LEVEL OF CONSCIOUSNESS
1. Does the patient respond to any of the following procedures (AVPU)?

A. Is he *awake*, aware, spontaneously speaking?
V. Does he respond to *verbal stimuli*, i.e. a loud call to 'Wake up!'?
P. Does he respond to *painful stimuli*, i.e. to a sharp pinch or slap?
U. Is he totally *unresponsive*?

E. EXPOSURE
The patient must be adequately exposed in order to examine him properly, so remove clothes as necessary.

NOW, SEND FOR HELP

If you think the patient's condition is serious following your assessment, you need to send or call for help from the emergency medical services (ambulance, paramedics). Whoever you send to get help should return to confirm that help is indeed on its way.

Recovery Position

If the patient is unconscious but breathing normally, there is a risk of vomiting and subsequent choking. It is therefore critical that the patient be turned onto his side in the recovery position.

1. Place the patient's right hand under his head with the palm forwards (facing up).

2. Cross the left leg over the right ankle.

3. Fold the left arm over the chest.

4. Grasp the left hip and pull the patient over onto his side with your right hand, supporting the patient's right cheek with the left hand.

5. Now flex the patient's left knee to 90°.

6. Flex the patient's left arm to 90° and place the forearm flat on the ground.

7. The patient is now in a stable recovery position.

If you suspect a spinal or neck injury be sure to immobilize the patient in a straight line before you turn him on his side.

Cardiopulmonary Resuscitation (CPR)

Cardiopulmonary resuscitation is required when a patient is found to have no pulse. It consists of techniques to:

• VENTILATE THE PATIENT'S LUNGS
  (EXPIRED AIR RESUSCITATION)
• PUMP THE PATIENT'S HEART
  (EXTERNAL CARDIAC COMPRESSION)

Once you have checked the ABCs (see Safety) you need to do the following:

A. AIRWAY
1. Gently extend the head (head tilt) and lift the chin with two fingers (chin lift). This will lift the tongue away from the back of the throat and open the airway.
2. If you suspect a foreign body in the airway sweep your finger across the back of the tongue from one side to the other. If an obstruction is found, remove it.

Do not attempt this on a conscious or semiconscious patient as they will either bite your finger off or vomit.

B. BREATHING
If the patient is not breathing you need to give expired air resuscitation, in other words, you need to breath into the patient's lungs:

1. Pinch the patient's nose closed.
2. Place your mouth, open, fully over the patient's mouth, making as good a seal as possible.
3. Exhale into the patient's mouth hard enough to cause the patient's chest to rise.
4. If the patient's chest fails to rise, you need to adjust the position of the airway. The 16% of oxygen in your expired air is adequate to sustain life.
5. Initially you need to give two full, slow breaths.
6. If the patient is found to have a pulse at this stage, continue breathing for the patient once every five seconds, checking for a pulse after every 10 breaths.
7. If the patient begins breathing on his own you can turn him into the recovery position.

C. CIRCULATION
After giving the two breaths as above you now need to give external cardiac compression.

1. Kneel next to the patient's chest.
2. Measure two finger breadths above the notch where the ribs meet the lower end of the breast bone.
3. Place the heel of your left hand just above your two fingers in the centre of the breast bone.
4. Place the heel of your right hand on your left hand.
5. Straighten your elbows.
6. Place your shoulders perpendicularly above the patient's breast bone.
7. Compress the breast bone 4-5cm to a rhythm of 'one, two, three...'.
8. Give 15 compressions.

Continue giving cycles of two breaths and 15 compressions, checking for a pulse after every five cycles.

The aim of CPR is to keep the patient alive until more sophisticated help arrives in the form of paramedics or a doctor with the necessary equipment. Make sure that you and your buddy are trained in CPR – it could mean the difference between life and death.

Diving Diseases and Illnesses

ACUTE DECOMPRESSION ILLNESS
Acute decompression illness means any illness arising out of the decompression of a diver, in other words, by the diver moving from an area of high ambient pressure to an area of lower pressure. It is divided into two groups:

• DECOMPRESSION SICKNESS
• BAROTRAUMA WITH ARTERIAL GAS EMBOLISM

It is not important for the diver or first-aider to differentiate between these two conditions because both are serious and both require the same emergency treatment. The important thing is to recognize acute decompression illness and to initiate emergency treatment.

The differences between decompression sickness and barotrauma are described below:

• DECOMPRESSION SICKNESS

Decompression sickness, or 'the bends', arises following inadequate decompression by the diver. Exposure to higher ambient pressure under water causes nitrogen to dissolve in increasing amounts in the body tissues. If this pressure is released gradually during correct and adequate decompression procedures the nitrogen escapes naturally into the blood and is exhaled through the lungs. If this release of pressure is too rapid the nitrogen cannot escape quickly enough and physical nitrogen bubbles form in the tissues.

The symptoms and signs of the disease are related to the tissues in which these bubbles form and the disease is described by the tissue affected, e.g. joint bend. Symptoms of decompression sickness include:

- Nausea and vomiting.
- Dizziness.
- Malaise and loss of appetite.
- Weakness.
- Joint pains or aches.
- Paralysis.
- Numbness.
- Itching of skin or skin rashes.
- Incontinence.
- Shortness of breath.

• BAROTRAUMA WITH ARTERIAL GAS EMBOLISM

Barotrauma refers to the damage that occurs when the tissue surrounding a gaseous space is injured following a change in the volume of air in that space.

An arterial gas embolism refers to a gas bubble that moves in a blood vessel usually leading to obstruction of that blood vessel or a vessel further downstream.

Barotrauma can therefore occur to any tissue that surrounds a gas-filled space, most commonly the:

• ears	middle ear squeeze	burst ear drum
• sinuses	sinus squeeze	sinus pain, nose bleeds
• lungs	lung squeeze	burst lung
• face	mask squeeze	swollen, bloodshot eyes
• teeth	tooth squeeze	toothache

A burst lung is the most serious of these and can result in arterial gas embolism. It occurs following a rapid ascent during which the diver does not exhale adequately. The rising pressure of expanding air in the lungs bursts the delicate alveoli, or lung sacs, and forces air into the blood vessels that carry blood back to the heart and ultimately

the brain. In the brain these bubbles of air block blood vessels and obstruct the supply of blood and oxygen to the brain, resulting in brain damage.

The symptoms of lung barotrauma and arterial gas embolism include:

- Shortness of breath.
- Chest pain.
- Unconsciousness or altered level of consciousness.
- Weakness, incoordination and paralysis.
- Blurred vision, loss of balance.

Treatment
1. ABCs (see Safety) and CPR as necessary.
2. Put the patient in the recovery position with no tilt or raising of the legs.
3. Administer 100% oxygen by mask (or demand valve).
4. Keep the patient warm.
5. Remove to the nearest hospital as soon as possible. The hospital or emergency services will arrange the recompression treatment required.

CARBON DIOXIDE OR
CARBON MONOXIDE POISONING

Carbon dioxide poisoning can occur as a result of:

- skip breathing – diver holds his breath on SCUBA
- heavy exercise on SCUBA
- malfunctioning rebreather systems

Carbon monoxide poisoning occurs as a result of:

- exhaust gases being pumped into cylinders
- hookah systems air intake too close to exhaust fumes

Symptoms would be:

- Headache.
- Blue colour of the skin.
- Shortness of breath.
- Decreased level of consciousness or loss of consciousness.

Treatment
1. ABCs (see Safety) as necessary.
2. CPR if required.
3. 100% oxygen through a mask or demand valve.
4. Remove to nearest hospital.

HEAD INJURY
All head injuries should at all times be regarded as potentially serious.

Treatment
The diver should surface and any wound should be disinfected. There should be no more diving until a doctor has been consulted.

If the diver is unconscious, the emergency services should be contacted. If breathing and/or pulse has stopped, CPR should be administered.

If the diver is breathing and has a pulse, check for bleeding and other injuries and treat for shock (*q.v.*); if wounds permit, put the sufferer into recovery position with no elevation of the legs and administer 100% oxygen. Keep him warm and comfortable, and monitor pulse and respiration constantly.

DO NOT administer fluids under any circumstances to an unconscious or semiconscious diver.

HYPERTHERMIA
(INCREASED BODY TEMPERATURE)
A rise in body temperature results from a combination of overheating, normally due to exercise, and inadequate fluid intake. The diver will progress through heat exhaustion to heat stroke with eventual collapse. Heat stroke is a serious illness and if the diver is not cooled and rehydrated immediately he can die.

Treatment
Remove the diver from the hot environment and remove all clothes. Sponge with a damp cloth and fan either manually or with an electric fan. If the patient is conscious, he can be given fluids orally.

If unconscious place him in the recovery position (*see* page 127) and monitor the ABCs. Always seek advanced medical help thereafter.

HYPOTHERMIA
Normal internal body temperature is just under 37°C (98.4°F). If for any reason it is pushed much below this – usually, in diving, through inadequate protective clothing – progressively more serious symptoms may occur, with death as the ultimate endpoint.

• A drop of 1°C (2°F) leads to shivering and discomfort.
• A 2°C (3°F) drop induces the body's self-heating mechanisms to react; blood flow to the peripheries is reduced and shivering becomes extreme.
• A 3°C (5°F) drop leads to amnesia, confusion, disorientation, heartbeat and breathing irregularities, and possibly rigor.

Treatment
• Move the patient to a sheltered, warm area or prevent further heat loss by wrapping him in a space blanket, surrounding the diver with your and your buddies' bodies, and covering his head and neck with a woolly hat, warm towels or anything suitable.
• In sheltered warmth, re-dress the diver in warm, dry clothing and then put him in a space blanket.
• If the diver is conscious and coherent, a warm shower or bath and a warm, sweet drink should be adequate treatment. If it isn't, call the emergency services and treat for shock while deploying the other warming measures noted.

NEAR DROWNING
Near drowning refers to a situation where the diver has inhaled some water. He may be conscious or unconscious. Water in the lungs interferes with the normal transport of oxygen from the lungs into the blood and near drowning victims are therefore often hypoxic.

Treatment
Remove the diver from the water and check the ABCs. Depending on your findings commence EAR (*see* Breathing under CPR page 127) or CPR where appropriate, beginning with EAR in the water if necessary. If possible administer oxygen by mask or demand valve.

All near drowning victims can develop secondary drowning at a later stage; this is a condition where fluid oozes into the lungs causing the diver to drown in his own secretions. All near drowning victims should, therefore, be observed for 24 hours in a hospital.

NITROGEN NARCOSIS
The air we breathe is about 80% nitrogen. Breathing the standard mixture under compression, as divers do, can lead to symptoms very much like those of drunkenness – giving rise to the popular term 'rapture of the deep'.

Some divers experience nitrogen narcosis at depths of 30-40m (100-130ft). Up to a depth of about 60m (200ft) – that is, beyond the legal maximum depth for sport diving in the UK, Mauritius and USA – the symptoms need not (but may) be serious; beyond about 80m (260ft) the diver may become unconscious. The onset of symptoms can be sudden and unheralded. The condition itself is not harmful; dangers arise through secondary effects, notably the diver doing something foolish.

Treatment
The only effective treatment is to return immediately to a shallower depth.

OXYGEN TOXICITY (POISONING)
Oxygen, if breathed at a partial pressure of greater than 1.5 atmospheres, can be poisonous to the lung and brain tissues.

• Lung toxicity is a more chronic event and is not commonly seen in sports divers.
• Brain toxicity is common and manifests when breathing pure (100%) oxygen at depths greater than 7msw (metres of sea water) or air deeper than 90msw.

The advent of Nitrox diving (increased oxygen percentage in the breathing mixture) will inevitably increase the incidence of brain oxygen toxicity. The clinical presentation of oxygen toxicity is sudden and unpredictable with unconsciousness and seizures which can be catastrophic under water.

Treatment
In the case of oxygen toxicity, prevention is definitely better than cure:

• Don't dive on 100% oxygen.
• Don't dive deeper than recommended for a particular Nitrox Mix.
• Don't dive deeper than 70m (250ft) on air.

SHOCK

Shock refers not to the emotional trauma of a frightening experience but to a physiological state in the body resulting from poor blood and oxygen delivery to the tissues. As a result of oxygen and blood deprivation the tissues cannot perform their functions.

There are many causes of shock, but the most common are loss of blood or hypovolaemic shock.

Treatment

Treatment is directed at restoring blood and oxygen delivery to the tissues, therefore maintain the ABCs and administer 100% oxygen. Control all external bleeding by direct pressure, pressure on pressure points and elevation of the affected limb. A tourniquet should only be used as a last resort, and only then on the arms and legs.

Unconscious, shocked victims should be placed on their side with the legs elevated.

GENERAL MARINE-RELATED AILMENTS

Apart from the specific diving-related illnesses the most common ailments divers are inflicted with include cuts and abrasions, coral cuts and stings, swimmer's ear, sea sickness, jellyfish stings and sunburn.

BITES FROM FEEDING FISH

Although fish-feeding is practised by some of the dive centre operators in Mauritius, it is done under controlled conditions and it can be dangerous as some fish can become aggressive. For example, sharks' feeding frenzies are uncontrollable, and sharks often bite light-coloured fins. Triggerfish can come at you very fast, and groupers and moray eels have nasty teeth. Napoleon wrasses have strong mouth suction and can bite. Even little Sergeant-majors can give your fingers a nasty nip.

Treatment

Be wary of feeding fish and of sticking your fingers into places into which you can't see. Wear gloves when diving.

CUTS AND ABRASIONS

Divers should wear appropriate abrasive protection for the environment. Prominent areas – hands, knees, elbows and feet – are most likely to be affected.

Treatment

The danger with abrasions is that they become infected, so all wounds should be thoroughly rinsed with water and an antiseptic such as hibitane in alcohol as soon as possible after the injury has occurred. Infection may progress to a stage where antibiotics are necessary. Spreading inflamed areas should receive medical attention.

SWIMMER'S EAR

Swimmer's ear is an infection of the external ear canal resulting from constantly wet ears. The infection is often a combination of a fungal and bacterial virus.

Treatment

Swimmer's ear can be prevented by always thoroughly drying the ears after diving and, if you are susceptible to the condition, by inserting alcohol or acetic acid drops after diving.

Never stick anything into your ear (including ear buds) as this will damage the normal lining and predispose the ear towards infection.

Once infected the best possible treatment is by halting diving or swimming activities for a few days and seeking medical advice.

If you are prone to swimmer's ear and are likely to be in a remote area, carry antibiotic drops with you as recommended by your diving physician.

SEA OR MOTION SICKNESS

Motion sickness can be an annoying complication on a diving holiday involving boat dives. If you are susceptible to motion sickness, seek medical advice prior to diving.

Treatment

To prevent sea sickness only eat light meals before going to sea and avoid alcohol the night before.

Normally a combination of metaclopamide (maxolon) and an antihistaminic (Valoid) or similar drugs can offer a simple preventative solution.

A cautionary note must be made that the antihistamine can make you drowsy, which may impair your ability to think and act while diving, so divers on antihistamines should limit their diving depth to less than 30m (100ft).

A seasick diver should not attempt to dive.

SUNBURN

The sun in Mauritius is particularly harsh.

Treatment

Divers are advised to wear appropriate wide-brimmed hats and protective clothing. High-protection-factor sun creams are recommended.

TROPICAL DISEASES

Yellow fever and malaria.

Treatment

Officially Mauritius only requires a yellow fever vaccination certificate for all travellers over one year in age who have come from an affected area.

Malaria only exists in the benign form (*P. virax*); it occurs throughout the year but only in some areas. Rodrigues is not a malaria area. Specialist advice on the correct anti-malarial prophylaxis can be obtained from your pharmacy or doctor.

Marine Animals that Bite

SHARKS

Sharks rarely attack divers but should always be treated with respect. Attacks are usually associated with the spearing of fish and the resultant vibrations and blood released into the water.

The Great white, uncommon as it is in Mauritian waters, is an exception to the rule. It has an unpredictable nature and should be avoided. Leave the water if a Great white makes an appearance. Seals are their normal prey but theories that divers are often mistaken as such fodder have not been disproven. Grey reef sharks can be very territorial. If a shark displays any agitated behaviour involving arching of the back and ventral pointing of the pectoral fins, this may be a sign of impending attack and the diver should leave the water.

Treatment

Injuries are normally severe and involve severe blood loss resulting in shock. Blood loss control is the main objective. Control bleeding by applying direct pressure to wounds, pressure on pressure points and by elevating the affected limb. Tourniquets (preferably a wide rubber bandage) may be used on limbs above an amputation.

The diver should be stabilized as far as possible with the available medical help before being transported as soon as possible to a hospital.

BARRACUDAS

Barracudas are usually seen in large safe shoals of several hundred fish, each up to 80cm (30in) long. Lone individuals about twice this size have been known to attack divers in tropical waters, usually in turbid or murky shallow water, where sunlight flashing off a knife blade, camera lens or jewellery has confused fish into thinking that they are attacking prey such as sardines. Serious incidents involving barracudas in Mauritius are unknown.

Treatment

Clean the wounds thoroughly and use antiseptic or antibiotic cream. Bad bites will need antibiotic and antitetanus treatment.

MORAY EELS

Probably, more divers are bitten by morays than by all other sea creatures added together – usually through divers putting their hands into holes to collect shells or lobsters, removing anchors or hiding baitfish. Often a moray eel, once it has a hold on you, refuses to let go. You can worsen the wound immensely by tearing your flesh as you try to pull the fish off, so rather attempt to persuade it to release its hold by using your knife.

Treatment

Thorough cleaning and, more often than not, stitches. The bites nearly always go septic, so have antibiotics and antitetanus available as a precautionary measure.

TRIGGERFISH

Large triggerfish – usually males guarding eggs in 'nests' – are particularly aggressive, and will attack divers who get too close. Their teeth are very strong, and can go through rubber fins and draw blood through a 4mm (1/6in) wetsuit.

Treatment

Clean the wound and treat it with antiseptic cream.

Marine Animals that Sting

Scorpionfish (*Scorpaenopsis gibbosa*), firefish (*Pterois miles*), Angler fish (*Antennarius* sp.) and stonefish (*Synancea verrucosa*) are the most common venomous fish. Many envenomed sea creatures are bottom-dwellers, hiding among coral or resting on or burrowing into sand. If you need to move along the sea bottom, do so in a shuffle, so that you push such creatures out of the way and minimize your risk of stepping directly onto their sharp, venomous spines, many of which can pierce rubber fins.

Antivenins require specialist medical supervision, do not work for all species and need refrigerated storage, so they are rarely available when required.

Most of the venoms are high-molecular-weight proteins that break down under heat. Immerse the limb in hot water (e.g. the cooling water from an outboard motor, if no other supply is available) at 50°C (120°F) for two hours, until the pain stops. Several injections of local anaesthetic (e.g. procain hydrochloride) around the wound will ease the pain.

Remember that venoms may still be active in fish that have been dead for 48 hours.

Younger or weaker victims may need CPR.

CONE SHELLS

A live cone shell (Conidae family) should never be handled. The animal has a mobile tube-like organ that shoots a poison dart. The result is initial numbness followed by local muscular paralysis, which may extend to respiratory paralysis and heart failure.

Treatment

Apply a broad ligature between the wound and the body. CPR and supportive care may be necessary.

CROWN-OF-THORNS STARFISH

The Crown-of-Thorns starfish (*Acanthaster planci*), has sharp spines that can even pierce gloves and break off under the skin, causing pain and sometimes nausea lasting several days.

Treatment

Apply the hot-water treatment (e.g. the cooling water from an outboard motor, if no other supply is available) at 50°C (120°F) for 30min, until the pain stops. Septic wounds require antibiotics.

FIRE CORAL

Fire corals (*Millespora* spp.) are more closely related to the stinging hydroids. Some people react violently to the slightest brush with them, and the resulting blisters may be 15cm (6in) across.

Treatment

Apply vinegar / acetic acid locally.

JELLYFISH

Most jellyfishes sting, but few are dangerous. As a general rule, those with the longest tentacles tend to have the most painful stings.

The box jellyfish or sea wasp and the blue bottle are the most common stingers encountered. Blue bottle and sea wasp stings can be treated with vinegar or alcohol which should be applied locally.

Divers commonly develop allergies to jellyfish and blue bottle stings and those sensitized should always carry a supply of antihistamines and, if necessary, their injection of adrenalin.

LIONFISH / TURKEYFISH / FIREFISH

These are slow-moving except when swallowing prey. They hang around on reefs and wrecks and pack a heavy sting in their beautiful spines.

Treatment

Use the hot water treatment, i.e. immerse the limb in hot water (e.g. the cooling water from an outboard motor, if no other supply is available) at 50°C (120°F) for two hours, until the pain stops.

Several injections of local anaesthetic (e.g. procain hydrochloride) around the wound will ease the pain.

Younger or weaker victims may need CPR.

SCORPIONFISH

Other scorpionfish are less camouflaged and less dangerous than the stonefish but are more common and quite dangerous enough.

Treatment

There is usually intense pain and swelling. Clean the wound, give the hot water treatment (immerse the limb in hot water, e.g. the cooling water from an outboard motor, if no other supply is available) at 50°C (120°F) for two hours, until the pain stops and follow up with antibiotic and antitetanus.

SEA URCHIN

The spines of sea urchins can be poisonous. Even if they aren't, they can puncture the skin, even through gloves, and break off, leaving painful wounds that can go septic.

Treatment

For bad cases of poisoning by a sea urchin's spine, give the hot water treatment (immerse the limb in hot water, e.g. the cooling water from an outboard motor, if no

other supply is available) at 50°C (120°F) for two hours, until the pain stops. This also serves to soften the spines, helping the body reject them. Several injections of local anaesthetic (e.g. procain hydrochloride) around the wound will ease the pain. Younger or weaker victims may need CPR. – *see* page 127).

Soothing creams or a magnesium-sulphate compress will help reduce the pain, as will the application of the flesh of papaya (paw-paw) fruit.

Alcohol applied after the heat might also prove useful. Septic wounds require antibiotics.

STINGING PLANKTON

You cannot see stinging plankton, and so cannot take evasive measures. If there are reports of any in the area, keep as much of your body covered as possible.

Treatment

Apply vinegar / acetic acid locally.

STINGRAYS

Stingrays vary from a few centimetres (in some parts of the world), to several metres across. The sting consists of one or more spines on top of the tail; though these point backwards they can sting in any direction. The rays thrash out and sting when trodden on or caught. Wounds may be large and severely lacerated.

Treatment

Clean the wound and remove any spines. Give the hot water treatment (immerse the limb in hot water, e.g. the cooling water from an outboard motor, if no other supply is available) at 50°C (120°F) for two hours, until the pain stops and apply local anaesthetic if available. Follow up with antibiotics and antitetanus.

STONEFISH

Stonefish are the most feared, best camouflaged and most dangerous of the scorpionfish family. The venom is contained in the spines of the dorsal fin, which is raised when the fish is agitated.

Treatment

There is usually intense pain and swelling resulting from an encounter with a stonefish.

Clean the wound, give the hot water treatment (immerse the limb in hot water, e.g. the cooling water from an outboard motor, if no other supply is available) at 50°C (120°F) for two hours, until the pain stops, and follow up with antibiotics and antitetanus.

MARINE ANIMALS THAT SHOCK

The one-fin electric ray is common in Mauritius and around the Indian Ocean islands, and is normally found on sandy bottoms. Contact with the ray will result in a powerful shock which could unsettle the diver sufficiently to cause an accident.

MARINE ANIMALS THAT ARE POISONOUS TO EAT

Eating shellfish can result in gastroenteritis, allergic reactions or paralytic shellfish poisoning. Avoid eating anything but fresh shellfish. If considering eating mussels, first find out from the local inhabitants if it is safe or if there has been a recent red tide.

Ciguatera poisoning can result from eating reef and game fish contaminated by a dinoflagellate. Obtain local advice on which fish are safe to eat. Avoid all but the freshest fish. Pufferfish and sunfish are not edible and ingestion of their flesh can result in death. Scromboid poisoning results from eating mackerel and tuna that have been allowed to lie in the sun.

DIVING RESCUE

One of the most common questions asked by divers is, 'What must I do if I find a buddy or another diver unconscious in the water?' Fortunately this is a rare occurrence as most diving incidents and accidents statistically happen on the surface.

The short answer to the question is that incidents and accidents should be avoided as far as possible, as a result of the following measures:

• Thorough training both initially and continuously in personal diving, rescue and emergency care skills.

• Maintaining good physical and mental fitness for diving and avoiding substances like alcohol and drugs which compromise that fitness.

• Equipment maintenance with regular servicing and checks to ensure reliable function.

• Familiarizing yourself with new equipment in the pool before using it in the sea.

• Diving with equipment appropriate to the complexity of the dive.

• Wearing appropriate thermal protection.

• Thorough pre-dive checks of equipment.

• Attention to buoyancy ensuring that you are not over- or underweight and that buoyancy control mechanisms are functioning normally.

• Detailed attention to thorough dive planning no matter how apparently routine the dive. Dive planning is an exercise in accident prevention.

If you find yourself in a situation where a diver requires active rescue, the situation can be managed in the following sequence:

1. DIVER RECOVERY
2. DIVER RESUSCITATION
3. DIVER EVACUATION

Diver recovery involves freeing the diver from any entrapment underwater and then providing buoyancy and lift to get him to the surface without further injury. The emphasis in getting the diver to the surface is on control of the ascent. The diver must be brought up from the dive in a controlled manner to avoid the possibility of barotrauma and air embolism.

To provide positive buoyancy it may be necessary to release the weight belt, inflate the victim's buoyancy compressor or inflate your own buoyancy compensator. A position behind the diver should be taken up with your right hand under the chin, keeping the airway open, and the other hand on the victim's BC inflator/deflator hose. Swim upward at a controlled moderate pace, being conscious of your own exhalation and a need not to become exhausted.

Once on the surface, resuscitation should begin in the water with expired air resuscitation while the diver is towed to the nearest boat or land where CPR can be initiated. Resuscitation is continued while preparations are made to evacuate the injured diver.

Treatment would include:

• EAR or CPR (see page 127) as necessary with or without the assistance of medical equipment.

• 100% oxygen by mask through a bag/valve/mask or demand valve.

• Keeping the diver warm.

• Maintaining hydration by intravenous therapy if skills and equipment are available.

Evacuation of the diver is by the quickest available means to the nearest resuscitation facility (or hospital trauma unit), the options being by sea, land or air, or a combination of all three.

The recompression treatment that may be required is arranged from the resuscitation facility once the diver has been adequately assessed.

Ignorance is your greatest enemy in a rescue situation and time and money spent on dive rescue training is an investment in life.

Approach your nearest agency for this type of training and before going for a dive find out what rescue facilities are available in the area of the dive and how they are contactable in an emergency.

RECOMPRESSION (HYPERBARIC) CHAMBER

There is only one facility in Mauritius, situated at the paramilitary Special Mobile Force at Vacoas. Make a note of the emergency number before diving.

Bibliography

ATCHIA, M. 1984. *Sea-fishes of Mauritius*. Forest-Side, Mauritius.

ADDISON, B. & TINDALL, J. 1990. *Coral Fishes of the Indian Ocean*. Southern Book Publishers, Halfway House.

BRANCH, G.M. & GRIFFITHS, C.L. 1994. *Two Oceans: A Guide to the Marine Life of Southern Africa*. David Philip, Cape Town.

CAMERON, R. 1961. *Shells*. Octopus Books Ltd., London.

KENNELLY, D.H. 1969. *Marine Shells of Southern Africa*. Books of Africa.

LIESKE, E. & MYER, R. 1994. *Coral Reef Fishes*. Harper Collins Publishers, London.

MUNGER, B. 1993. *An Invitation to the Charms of Mauritian Localities*. Vacoas, Mauritius.

ROBERTS, K. & E. 1992. *Mauritius, Rodrigues and Réunion*. Moorland Publishing Co. Ltd., Ashbourne, England.

SMITH, J.L.B. 1977. *Smith's Sea Fishes*. Valiant Publishers, Sandton.

STRAUSS, R. & SWANEY, D. 1993 (2nd edition). *Mauritius, Réunion and Seychelles: A Travel Survival Kit*. Lonely Planet Publications, Australia.

VAN DER ELST, R. 1981. *A Guide to the Common Sea Fishes of Southern Africa*. C. Struik, Cape Town.

VENTER, A.J. 1989. *Underwater Mauritius*. Ashanti Publishing Ltd., Gibraltar.

WALKER, I. 1993. *The Complete Guide to the Southwest Indian Ocean*. Cornelius Books, Port Angolès.

ZANELLI, L. (Ed.) 1975 (8th edition). *British Sub Aqua Club Diving Manual*. Hants.

Index

Individual dive sites are represented in **bold**